America and Her Influence upon the Language
and Culture of Post-socialist Countries

FREIBERGER BEITRÄGE
zum Einfluß der angloamerikanischen Sprache und Kultur auf Europa
Herausgegeben von Hermann Fink und Liane Fijas

Band 5

PETER LANG
Frankfurt am Main · Berlin · Bern · New York · Paris · Wien

Hermann Fink
Liane Fijas
(Hrsg.)

America
and Her Influence
upon the Language
and Culture
of Post-socialist
Countries

PETER LANG
Europäischer Verlag der Wissenschaften

Die Deutsche Bibliothek - CIP-Einheitsaufnahme

America and her influence upon the language and culture of
post-socialist countries / Hermann Fink ; Liane Fijas (Eds.). -
Frankfurt am Main ; Berlin ; Bern ; New York ; Paris ; Wien :
Lang, 1998
    (Freiberger Beiträge zum Einfluß der angloamerikanischen
    Sprache und Kultur auf Europa ; Bd. 5)
    ISBN 3-631-33193-2

ISSN 1431-2220
ISBN 3-631-33193-2
US-ISBN 0-8204-3577-5

© Peter Lang GmbH
Europäischer Verlag der Wissenschaften
Frankfurt am Main 1998
All rights reserved.

Printed in Germany 1 2 3 4   6 7

Inhaltsverzeichnis

Vorwort

Im Namen der *Sprachwerkstatt*, einer per Definition Sprachen und menschlicher Kommunikation eng verbundenen und gewidmeten Bildungseinrichtung, freue ich mich, als deren Geschäftsführer, die Herausgabe eines weiteren, auf die Interferenzen des Amerikanisch-Englischen bezogenen Bandes - dieses Mal der „Freiberger Beiträge zum Einfluß der angloamerikanischen Sprache und Kultur auf Europa" - finanziell ermöglichen zu können.

Von besonderem Interesse und von großer Bedeutung erachte ich dabei, daß sich das vorliegende Büchlein auf den Amerikanismus in den nunmehr der westlichen Welt und ihrem freien Marktwirtschaftssystem geöffneten, ehemals dem ungehinderten Gedankenaustausch aber verschlossenen sozialistischen Ländern bezieht. Dies umso mehr als die *Sprachwerkstatt* sich seit Öffnung der Grenzen in besonderem Maß durch die Errichtung von Bildungseinrichtungen in Ostdeutschland sowie eines Gymnasiums und einer Wirtschaftshochschule in Polen erfolgreich bemüht hat, den Kommunikations- und kulturellen Austauschprozeß unter Wahrung und Erhaltung der jeweiligen regionalen und nationalen kulturellen Identität zu fördern.

Die Befürchtungen, daß diese soziale, kulturelle und sprachliche Identität durch die Amerikanisierung Europas und der Welt schlechthin verloren gehen, zumindestens aber gleichgemacht und verflacht werden könnte, gehen aus den Beiträgen in diesem Buch zu den Verhältnissen in Rußland, Estland, der Tschechischen Republik und Slowakeien deutlich hervor. Insofern freuen wir uns, die Erforschung der modernen Tendenzen der gegenwärtigen gesellschaftlichen und kulturellen sowie sprachlichen Entwicklungen im Osten Europas unterstützen zu können.

Paderborn, Leipzig, Dresden und Breslau, im Winter 1997

Hubert Tiez, M.A.
Die Sprachwerkstatt
Privates Institut für Kommunikation,
Wirtschaft und Sprache GmbH

Zum Inhalt

Der bereits seit dem letzten Jahrhundert andauernde Einfluß des Englischen, und nach dem 2. Weltkrieg vornehmlich dessen nordamerikanischer Variante, auf das Deutsche ist im Grunde nichts Neues. In der Literatur wurde vor allem die lexikalische Aufnahme von Englischem in das Deutsche reichlich dokumentiert. Nach Veröffentlichungen, wie der von Agnes Bain Stiven (Englands Einfluß auf den deutschen Wortschatz, Zeulenroda, 1936), schon vor dem 2. Weltkrieg, die bereits den starken amerikanischen Einfluß und die Schwierigkeit der Differenzierung zwischen Britizismus und Amerikanismus herausstellte, entstanden Untersuchungen dieser Interferenzerscheinung, vor allem im Nachkriegswesten, in erster Linie für die deutsche Sprache und die französische (man denke nur an René Etiemble mit seinem Parlez-vous franglais ?, Paris 1964), aber nicht nur für diese, in den „Pionierarbeiten" von Peter Ganz (Der englische Einfluß auf den deutschen Wortschatz 1640 - 1815, Berlin 1957), Horst Zindler (Anglizismen in der deutschen Presse nach 1945, Diss., Kiel, 1959), Broder Carstensen (Englische Einflüsse auf die deutsche Sprache nach 1945), Heidelberg, 1965), Hermann Fink (Amerikanismen im Wortschatz der deutschen Tagespresse, dargestellt am Beispiel dreier überregionaler Zeitungen (Süddeutsche Zeitung, Frankfurter Allgemeine Zeitung, Die Welt)), Mainzer Amerikanistische Beiträge 11, München 1970), Hans Galinsky, dem Nestor der Nachkriegsamerikanistik in Deutschland (Amerikanisch-englische und Gesamtenglische Interferenzen mit dem Deutschen und anderen Sprachen der Gegenwart. Ein kritischer Forschungsbericht 1945 - 1976, in Kolb, Herbert und Lauffer, Hartmut (Hrsg.), Sprachliche Interferenz; Festschrift für Werner Betz zum 65. Geburtstag, Tübingen, 1977, 463 - 517), Karin Viereck (Englisches Wortgut, seine Häufigkeit und Integration in der österreichischen und bundesdeutschen Pressesprache, Bamberger Beiträge zur englischen Sprachwissenschaft 8, Frankfurt a.M., 1980), bis hin zur verhältnismäßig frühen, damals bereits den Spracheinfluß sehr kritisch, wenn nicht sogar sprachpuristisch sehenden Arbeit von Wolfram Wilss („Der Einfluß der englischen Sprache auf die deutsche seit 1945", Beiträge zur Linguistik und Informationsverarbeitung 8, 1966, 30 - 48), um nur einige, neben vielen anderen verdienstvollen hier zu nennen.

Die bisher erschienen Bände der Reihe „America and Her Influence upon the Languages and Cultures of Post-socialist Countries" haben sich explizit mit dem linguistischen Einfluß des Angloamerikanischen auf die deutsche Sprache der ehemaligen Deutschen Demokratischen Republik und nornehmlich mit der aus dem Englischen entlehnten Lexik befaßt und dabei auch gelegentlich die sozialen und psychologischen Auswirkungen, d.h. deren kulturelle Tragweite anklingen lassen. Der von Kulturkritikern und auch Linguisten schon seit Jahrzehnten in der Bundesrepublik oft beschworene und manchmal auch als Kulturimperialismus der Vereinigten Staaten bezeichnete kulturelle Einfluß, wurde dabei aber nur am Rande besprochen.

So ist tatsächlich der bei Wills schon vor über drei Jahrzehnten implizierte, in Leserbriefen und journalistischen Traktaten, z.B. von Dieter E. Zimmer in „Die Zeit" gelegentlich angesprochene und in Frankreich schon indirekt per Gesetz „geregelte", bei uns kürzlich im Schreiben eines bei den europäischen Behörden in einem Benelux-Land tätigen Übersetzers deutscher Muttersprache bitter angemahnte („*Wenn man sich mit seiner Sprache identifiziert, darf der Ton ausnahmsweise vielleicht einmal bitter sein*") Aspekt „*Das Anwachsen der Erscheinung* [Anglizismen und Amerikanismen im Deutschen] *macht es m.E. jetzt erforderlich, über ihre wissenschaftliche Beschreibung und Registrierung hinaus Stellung zu beziehen!*" wissenschaftlich nur mit geringer Intensität untersucht worden. Und wo Bemerkungen zu den tatsächlichen oder möglichen sozialen, ökonomischen, philosophischen, psychologischen, politischen und kulturellen Implikationen der für den Alltagsmenschen offensichtlich kaum bemerkbaren, zumindest nicht bewußt registrierten tiefergehenden Folgen des Spracheinflusses gefallen sind, waren sie in der Tat meistens entweder sprachpuristisch oder politisch polemisch - man vergleiche nur die doch schon antiamerikanistisch anmutenden Bände von Rolf Winter (Ami go home, Hamburg, 1992, Der amerikanische Alptraum, München 1992; Die amerikanische Zumutung, München 1991; oder Gottes eigenes Land, Hamburg 1991) - oder entbehrten der gesicherten empirischen Grundlage. Bei unserer Bitte an Kollegen in anderen als den deutschen Neuen Ländern von der „Wende" betroffenen ehemaligen sozialistischen Sprachgemeinschaften, sich zu „America and Her Influence upon the Languages and Cultures of the Post-socialist Countries" zu äußern, erwarteten wir den allgemeinen Tenor der sprachwissenschaftlichen, fast ausschließlich lexikbezogenen Abhandlung.

Wie die Beiträge zeigen, sieht man jedoch den angloamerikanischen Einfluß offensichtlich nicht so sehr als ein das Sprachsystem berührendes Problem oder eine Bereicherung, sondern eher sozial- und kulturkritisch.

So eröffnet *Maria Pešeková den Band,* humorvoll und ironisch, mit „IST ALLES, WAS AMERIKANISCH IST, SUPER?", einer eher kritisch analytischen Betrachtung der Ver- und Ausbreitung der amerikanischen Kultur in der Slowakei von frühen Ansätzen zur Zeit der Industrialisierung, bis zu den schwerwiegenden Folgen der gesellschaftlichen Veränderung in Mitteleuropa im Jahre 1989.

Daran schließt die Untersuchung des AE-Einflusses in der nach dem Umschwung neu gegründeten unabhängigen Tschechischen Republik an. Unter „AMERICA AND HER INFLUENCE ON THE CZECH REPUBLIC" stellt *Otilia Venková* Betrachtungen an zum sprachlichen Einfluß und, darauf basierend, zum amerikanischen Einfluß, u.a. auf Lebenstil, Geschäftsleben, Kommunikation, Beschäftigung, Massenmedien, Mode und Familie, nicht zuletzt auch im Sinne einer daraus entstehenden Verdeutlichung, Betonung und Hervorhebung der eigenen Sprache und Kultur.

Aus der noch relativ frischen Erfahrung eines Amerika-Aufenthaltes beurteilt *Marcela Adámková* den Einfluß auf die heutige Tschechische Gesellschaft unter dem Titel „AMERICA IS TOUGH BUT ENGLIGHTENING" mit der einleitenden Feststellung, daß die

Tschechische Lebensweise sich nach der „Velvet Revolution" dramatisch geändert hat, um sodann die Rolle Amerikas und die Auswirkungen des amerkanischen Englisch in ihrer Sprache in solchen Bereichen wie z.b. „economics, sports, fashion, mass media, travel, politics, money, job and succes, family life", und „family policy", mit einer abschließenden kritischen Bemerkung des fremden Einflusses darzustellen.

In erfrischender Weise, fast satirisch-drastisch und auf tiefgreifende identitätsverändernde Folgen hinweisend, bietet *Mari Uibo* unter „AMERICAN CULTURE IN ESTONIA" einen kultur- und sozialkritischen Überblick zur Entwicklung Estlands in der Kontrastierung von „Estonia, the Way It Used to Be", „Estonia Today", „Education" und „Pop Culture", bis zu „Social Behavior", „The Cult of Money", „Manners and Morals", und der im Land eingezogenen „Keep Smiling"-Lebensart.

Selbst der darauffolgende sehr knappe, sprachensystembezogene Fragen des Englischen im Slowakischen behandelnde Beitrag von *Viera Nemčoková* „ENGLISH COMPUTING TERMS IN THE SLOVAK LANGUAGE" eröffnet die Betrachtung der Rolle der Vereinigten Staaten mit der Feststellung „This use of foreign language register [d.h. des Englischen] as an integral part of the Slovak language .... reflects the deep-reaching linguistic, social, and cultural impact America has made upon post-socialist Slovakia".

Die erhebliche Tiefenwirkung Amerikas auf das slowakische Bildungssystem, insbesonders auf das Lehren von Englisch als Fremdsprache nach dem Kollaps des Sozialismus, betrachtet *Gabriela Knutová* in ihrem Beitrag „ENGLISH AS A FOREIGN LANGUAGE IN POST-SOCIALIST SLOVAKIA". Durch Gegenüberstellung der

Verhältnisse vor diesem Fall (politischer Druck der Sowjetunion) und der quasi demokratischen Hereinwahl Amerikas in das System der nunmehr in der Slovakei gelehrten Fremdsprachen, legt sie deutlich Zeugnis ab von den enormen, unter britischem, vor allem aber unter US-amerikanischem Einfluß, politisch freien und marktwirtschaftlich orientierten bildungspolitischen Veränderungen. Zugleich warnt sie aber auch vor den damit verbundenen negativen kulturellen Folgen.

Den Abschluß bilden vornehmlich sprachbezogene Beobachtungen von *Liane Fijas* zum Gesamtthema unter dem Titel „ZUM ENGLISCHEN EINFLUß AUF DAS HEUTIGE RUSSISCH UND TSCHECHISCH". Sie beschreibt, anhand von Beispielen, die Anfang der 90er Jahre begründete Umorientierung der Anglizismen im Russischen von der ideologischen negativ markierten Lexik zur zweckbestimmten Terminologie in den Entlehnungstypen und -verfahren sowie Bereichen. Auch sie zitiert die kritischen Stimmen einer russischen Wissenschaftlerin, z.B. mit dem Zitat „Anglizismen beginnen die Rolle destruktiver Elemente zu spielen, die den Sprachcode unterminieren" und bemerkt, daß es in Rußland kaum Bestrebungen gibt, die rasante Aufnahme von Anglizismen in die Sprache zu bremsen. In einem kurzen Exkurs belegt sie zu den formalsprachlichen Integrationsformen und -weisen von Anglizismen schon in anderen Beiträgen gemachte Aussagen zum Einfluß des AE auf das Tschechische.

Insgesamt beweisen die Aufsätze, daß Amerika nicht nur in den Idiomen des gesamten ehemaligen Ostblocks (der aus Polen versprochene Beitrag blieb leider aus), sondern auch bereits tief in Lebensweise, Wirtschaft Kultur und Politiken der ehemaligen Satelliten der Sowjetunion eingedrungen und darin verankert ist, und nicht wenige befürchten, daß die so häufig als amerikanische Kulturinvasion apostrophierte McDonaldisierung im wahrsten Sinne des Wortes auch schon für diesen Teil der Welt gesichert ist.

IST ALLES WAS AMERIKANISCH IST, SUPER!?
Mária Pešeková

Die Soziologen sind schon vor langer Zeit zur Erkenntnis gekommen, daß die ungleichmäßige Entwicklung einzelner Gesellschaften die Verbreitung der Kultur ermöglicht. Im Prozeß dieser Verbreitung dringen aus den entwickelten Gesellschaften bestimmte Elemente und Komplexe durch, welche die Entwicklung einer anderen Gesellschaft beeinflussen. Dadurch verkürzt die Verbreitung der Kultur den natürlichen Weg der gesellschaftlichen Entwicklung.

Die Durchdringung einer Kultur geschieht mittels verschiedenartiger Instrumente, so auch durch Kontakte zwischen Individuen. Dabei werden Ideen, Gewohnheiten, Bücher, neue künstlerische und wissenschaftliche Erkentnisse und vieles andere übertragen.
Zu einer ähnlichen Übertragung kommt es auch durch Kontakte zwischen unterschiedlichen Institutionen, durch Handel, durch den Aufbau von Kommunikations- und Verkehrssystemen.
Im Vorbereitungsprozeß werden die materiellen Elemente schneller übertragen als die nicht-materiellen. Die Randelemente der abgebenden Kultur, die weniger mit dem Gefüge und der gesellschaftlichen Organisation der aufnehmenden Gemeinschaft verbunden sind, werden schneller aufgenommen als die Kernelemente einer Kultur. So nehmen primitive Völker den Schmuck und die Bekleidung einer entwickelten Kultur leichter auf, als die Arbeitsinstrumente, die die eingelaufenen Arbeitsgänge verändern würden.

Es kommt vor, daß zu Zeiten plötzlicher gesellschaftlicher Veränderungen, wenn das Einhalten des geeigneten Entwicklungstempos zum bedeutenden politischen Problem wird, von der Gesellschaft oder von bestimmten Gruppen besondere Institutionen gebildet werden, deren

Aufgabe die Unterstützung der Kultur und die Erleichterung der Aufnahme und Integration von Kulturwerten anderer Kulturen ist.

Wie verläuft nun die Ver- und Ausbreitung der amerikanischen Kultur in der Slowakei? Oder, besser noch, welchen Einfluß hat die amerikanische Kultur auf die heutige Slowakei?

Die Geschichte dieses Prozesses hat irgendwann am Anfang unseres Jahrhunderts begonnen. Deutlichere Merkmale erlangte sie in der Zeit der Entstehung der Tschechoslowakischen Republik aus den Trümmern der ehemaligen großen k. u. k. österreich-ungarischen Monarchie. Hunger und Armut zwangen zu jener Zeit viele Slowaken, nach Amerika auszuwandern. Sie gingen weg in der Hoffnung, dort das tägliche Brot zu verdienen. Sie waren meistens einfache Dorfleute, die kein Englisch sprechen konnten. Sie waren aber bescheiden und schwere Arbeit gewohnt. Deshalb haben sich auch viele im fremden Land durchgesetzt. Die Familienbindungen in der Slowakei waren sehr stark und die Auswanderer vergaßen ihre Leute zu Hause nicht. Ab und zu schickten sie ein paar Dollar nach Hause.

In armen Ländern hatte damals der Dollar - und das gilt bis heute - eine magische Macht. Er wurde zum Symbol des Reichtums der amerikanischen Gesellschaft.
Auch wenn die Dorfleute in den 20er und 30er Jahren unseres Jahrhunderts nichts als Armut und schwere Arbeit kannten, gelangte der Dollar als Schlüssel zum fabelhaften Leben in ihre Sehnsüchte und Träume.

Zur Zeit der ersten Tschechoslowakischen Republik (1918-1939) gab es in Zlín einen bedeutenden tschechischen Unternehmer, den Schuhhersteller Tomáš Bata.

Auch er wurde von Amerika beeinflußt, und lernte die Theorie und Erkentnisse von F. W. Taylor kennen, dem das amerikanische "time is money" nachgesagt wird. Taylor, von dem deutschen Soziologen Max Weber und seiner sozialen Theorie der Rationalisierung inspiriert, wurde der Begünder des wissenschaftlichen Managements. Er konzentrierte sich auf die volle Ausnutzung der Arbeitszeit, auf die Leistung und auf die Entlohnung der Angestellten nach Leistung. Er arbeitete ein genaues Netz organisatorischer Hinweise und Anordnungen aus, in dem der Angestellte nur ein Rädchen im riesigen Produktionsmechanismus wurde.

Bata hatte die Inspiration bei Henry Ford und in seinem System der Arbeitsorganisation gefunden. Er war begeistert von Fords Idee, daß "das Unternehmen ein Dienst für die Öffentlichkeit sei" und von seiner grundlegenden Philosophie überzeugt, das Bemühen, die technischen Erfindungen besser zu nützen, den Angestellten die Arbeit zu erleichtern, die Kosten der Arbeit zu minimieren, die Produktion zu erhöhen und die Preise zu senken. Bata wurde zwar vom Taylorismus und Fordismus, d.h. von „Amerikanismen" beeinflußt, er konzipierte aber auf der Grundlage dieser Erkentnisse sein eigenes System der Arbeitsorganisation, den Batismus.

In diesem System steht an erster Stelle der Mensch; der Mensch als Angestellter des Wirtschaftsunternehmens und der Mensch als Kunde. Auf die von Bata mittels seines Slogans "Unser Kunde - unser Herr" eingeführte Praxis, legen auch heute moderne Firmen großen Wert. Auch das ist ein Beispiel der Verbreitung amerikanischer Kultur bei uns und ein Kapitel in den Beziehungen zwischen den Vereinigten Staaten und unserem Land.

9

Das Bild des modernen Europas, vor allem Mitteleuropas, entstand aus einem Wirrwarr der Ereignisse des 2. Weltkrieges. Das Treffen von zwei gewaltigen Siegerarmeen auf dem Haufen der Schmerzen und des Leidens der Menschen beeinflußten den Weg, den Europa nach dem Krieg ging.

Durch die Ablehnung des Marshall-Plans fiel die Tschechoslowakei in diese Arme des sowjetischen Bruders und die Umarmung war fest und kräftig; zu einem kurzen Aufatmen kam es erst 1968 unter Alexander Dubcec.

Die Päckchen und Pakete von den Verwandten aus den USA und die CARE-Pakete, die noch in den fünfziger Jahren in die Slowakei kamen, enthielten unvorstellbare Sachen! Kaugummi und Nylonstrümpfe! Aber was soll ein Kaugummi, wenn der Mensch Hunger hat?
Es muß aber etwas großartiges und luxuriöses und außerdem wohl auch wertvolles gewesen sein! Es kam doch aus Amerika! Der Kaugummi wurde bis zum totalen Zerfallen gekaut. Weggeworfen wurde er erst, wenn er zu einer unanschaulichen klebrigen Masse geworden war. Die Amerikaner wären schockiert gewesen, wenn sie gesehen hätten, wie mit einer solchen Nichtigkeit - mit einem amerikanischen Kaugummi - in jener Zeit umgegangen wurde.

Ein ähnliches Verhältnis zum amerikanischen Kaugummi habe ich noch 1990 in Rußland erlebt. Ich flog von Moskau nach Sotschi. Meine Nachbarin im Flugzeug war eine "Babuschka" (alte Frau) aus Sachalin. Sie wollte mir etwas besonderes wertvolles schenken. Aus dem Gepäck zog sie einen Kaugummi und betonte, daß sie mir das wertvollste schenkte, was sie hatte - einen amerikanischen Kaugummi.

Ein anderes Wunder aus Amerika, das in den fünfziger Jahren die Männer und Frauen faszinierte, waren Nylonstrümpfe. Diese Pracht und Feinheit, dieser Glanz und diese Eleganz. Ja, das war Amerika! So etwas konnte nur in Amerika hergestellt werden. Nur schade, daß sie zu schnell rissen. Die Nylonstrümpfe - unwiderstehlich, zart und geschmeidig! Eine Illusion von Luxus, Schönheit und Sehnsucht. Das mußte ein wundervolles Land sein, wo die Frauen solche Strümpfe tragen konnten. Vielleicht war auch das Leben dort so wundervoll und leicht!

In der Tschechoslowakei erlebten wir politische Prozesse, fingen mit der Kollektivierung der Landwirtschaft an. Voll Begeisterung waren wir auf dem Weg zum Sozialismus. Unser großer Bruder, die Sowjetunion, würde bald die größte Menge Stahl pro Kopf produzieren.
Der Sozialismus fing mit anderen Mitteln die Leute ein! Sie wurden durch andere, eigene, dem System eigene Methoden und Instrumente erobert. Schönheit und Eleganz waren im Grund gar nicht so wichtig.

„Amerika ist eine andere Welt", behaupteten die vom US-Kongreß finanzierten Sender „Stimme Amerikas" und „Radio Freies Europa". Die Massenmedien überwanden leicht Raum und Zeit. Sogar die vollkommenste Berliner Mauer konnte nicht verhindern, daß im sozialistischen Lager die Ideen der Freiheit und der Demokratie durchdrangen.
Auf den Ätherwellen gelangten zu uns Informationen über Ereignisse, die bei uns zu Hause geschahen. Diese Nachrichten boten aber ein ganz anderes Bild. Es wurde offen über die Freiheit gesprochen. Das hat uns fasziniert, begeistert, bedrückt, empört und gleichzeitig mit Hoffnung erfüllt.

Im Jahre 1989 geschahen dann bedeutende gesellschaftliche Veränderungen in ganz Mitteleuropa.

Endlich! Der Traum über Amerika, „the American Dream", war näher gekommen. Er war fast zum Greifen nahe. Er erforderte nur ganz wenig - Geld zu haben und englisch zu sprechen. Wenn aber eines von beiden fehlte, entfernte sich der Traum wieder. Das wunderschöne Land, über das wir so viele Illusionen geschaffen hatten, floh wieder von uns. Oder doch nicht?

Amerikanische Firmen sind bereit, Europa zu erobern. Der Angriff ist gut überlegt, ein klares Ziel ist gesetzt, die Strategie ist überprüft. Sie kommen auch in die Slowakei. Wörter wie "Dealer" und "Marketing" werden sofort in die selbstverständlichen Instrumente täglicher Kommunikation eingegliedert und signalisieren, daß die Beziehung zu Amerika nicht mehr romantisch ist, sondern vom Marktmechanismus diktiert wird.

Amerika in der Slowakei! Coca Cola, Pepsi Cola, Procter and Gamble, Ford, McDonald's, Amway, Johnson and Johnson und viele andere Amerikanismen machen sich breit.

Mit den amerikanischen Firmen ist auch die amerikanische Werbung zu uns gekommen. Ach, wie wäre es so schön, noch einmal zwanzig zu sein, bis ans Ende der Welt zu segeln, mit den schönsten Mädchen ins Wasser zu springen. Die Reklame ist voll von lächelnden und glücklichen Menschen, die ihre Probleme lösen, indem sie ein neues Haarschampoo, Uncle Ben's Reis oder einen Ford kaufen.

Die Reklame zwingt uns im Unterbewußtsein diese Welt auf, die uns davon überzeugen soll, daß Jugend, Gesundheit, Zufriedenheit und Vollkommenheit, sowie unser Elan von der von uns gekauften Ware abhängig sind.

"Die Reklame verkauft Glück", behaupten unentwegt die großen Magier der modernen Gesellschaft.

Aber wer möchte nicht reich und glücklich werden? Die Amerikaner überzeugen uns, daß es einfach ist reich zu werden. Wirklich? Vielleicht genügt es nur einen Spaziergang über den Broadway zu machen und das dort auf der Straße herumliegende Geld aufzusammeln. Oder nicht? Oder wenigstens eine gute Stelle in einer amerikanischen Firma zu bekommen. Vielleicht kann man dort einen Schatz entdecken.

Ein Student, der ein paar Monate bei Coca Cola arbeitete, kommentierte die dortige Situation: "Alle duzen sich, lächeln sich gegenseitig an. Ich hatte das Gefühl, daß sie etwas vorspielen."
Dieses Verhaltensvorbild, akzeptiert und selbstverständlich in der amerikanischen Gesellschaft, wirkt fremd unter unseren Bedingungen und in unserer Gesellschaft.

Coca Cola stellt das Symbol des Kapitalismus, des Lebens, der amerikanischen Rasanz dar. Coca Cola hat die ganze Welt erobert. Diese Firma braucht nichts zu versprechen, zu überzeugen, neue Ideen zu bringen. Es reicht, das Logo aufzukleben und uns zu hypnotisieren! Coca Cola - das ist die reiche Konsumgesellschaft.

Die amerikanische Firma Amway hat in vielen ehemaligen sozialistischen Ländern Fuß gefaßt - in Ungarn, in der Tschechischen Republik und auch in der Slowakei. Eine überlegte und raffiniert ausgearbeitete Strategie massiert gründlich das Gehirn und die Geldbörse des Kunden und des „Dealers". Und das Ergebnis? In kurzer Zeit werden auch Sie wie Amway denken, auch Sie werden sich wie Amway verhalten und Ihre Welt wird nur noch Amway sein. Sie werden sich Ihre Freunde nach der Anzahl von gekauften Amway-Produkten auswählen und sie nach dem Verkaufserfolg beurteilen. Möchten Sie etwas von der Firma haben - bezahlen Sie dafür!

Amerikanische Unternehmer denken in Dollar; sie können alles in Dollar umwandeln. Auch das werden wir bald von ihnen lernen. Die Firma Amway wird sicher dazu ihren maßgeblichen Anteil beitragen.

Es ist ein Widerspruch, daß wir in unserer Gesellschaft nur die teuer bezahlten Werte hoch schätzen. Den Wert der Freiheit, die wir so leicht bekommen haben, schätzen wir dagegen nur gering.
In einer Umfrage sollten Studenten die fünf im Leben meistgeschätzten Werte angeben. Von 58 befragten Studenten im dritten Semester der Technischen Universität Košice, gaben nur zwei die Freiheit an!

So werden wir leicht zu Sklaven der großen Firma Amerika, die uns eine reiche Belohnung verspricht. Es sieht so aus, als ob wir in der Slowakei uns nicht ein demokratisch-funktionierendes Gesellschaftsmodell wünschen, so wie es in USA besteht. Was wir wollen, ist nur konsumieren, so wie die reichen Amerikaner.

Die Mutigsten unter uns glauben, daß Arbeit von früh am Morgen bis spät am Abend das Glück auf amerikanische Weise bringt. Sie opfern ihrer Unternehmenstätigkeit alles: Ihre Ideen, ihre Gesundheit, ihre Familie, ihre Freunde.
Die Arbeit in der Firma und für die Firma ist zur Droge geworden, ohne die die Menschen nicht leben können.
Das Problem des Workalismus kennen in der Slowakei nicht nur die Psychologen, sondern auch die heranwachsenden Kinder der Unternehmer. Workalismus bringt nicht Glück, sondern den Zerfall der Familie.
Wir wünschen uns doch so sehr - möglichst bald - in der Slowakei „Amerika" zu haben! Allein der Gedanke daran ist so unwiderstehlich, so anziehend.

Wir tragen T-Shirts mit großer Aufschrift „USA Today", Jeans und Sportschuhe, wir trinken Coca Cola, Pepsi Cola, Whisky und kauen Wrigley's Kaugummi. Wir rauchen amerikanische Zigaretten, verwenden nur amerikanische Kosmetik, amerikanische Reinigungsmittel; im Haus haben wir einen IBM-Rechner und vor dem Haus den Ford.

Wir setzen uns in den Sessel und legen die Beine auf den Tisch. Wie in Amerika! Im Fernsehen bewundern wir mit Spannung die Taten von Superman, oder starken Männern, die voller Tapferkeit und Selbstlosigkeit blauäugige blonde Mädchen im kalifornischen Santa Monica retten. Wir sind gerührt von Geschichten der goldenen Jugend in Beverly Hills.

Wir möchten O.K. und happy sein! Das Wunder geschieht aber nicht... Wir sind nicht happy und wir fühlen uns nicht O.K., obwohl wir ab und zu einen Big Mac bei McDonald' s kaufen...

Aber die Probleme lösen sich nicht von selbst und das Glück kommt eben nicht automatisch.

Welcher Weg führt zu einer Gesellschaft freier, schöpferischer und zufriedener Menschen? The American Way? Oder bleibt auch der nur ein American Dream?

AMERICA AND HER INFLUENCE ON THE CZECH REPUBLIC

Otilia Venkovà

1. Indroduction

A thorough study of America´s influence on the Czech language, the Czech culture, and the way of life in the Czech Republic (CR) would require long-lasting research. In fact, since for whatever reasons, historical, political or economic, the USA has become the most dominating country in the world this influence has been a continuous and permanent process. Since researching this phenomenon presumes ongoing investigation, it can hardly ever be completed.

This paper does not claim to be a complete scholarly study. As a matter of fact, it is merely a summary of information from my personal experience, views, observations, studies and reading. It presents authentic materials gathered from real-life situations. As such, the work should be considered only a first orientation for further research and analysis.

2. A Brief Look Back

Until the end of World War II the study of American English and the impact of America upon culture and language was largely neglected in Europe. Often English language dictionaries did not even reflect the usage of American English. But due to the development and influence of American science and technology, civilization, trade, export and air traffic control, the English language - and increasingly its American variety, has become international and a lingua franca for the entire world.

The task of this contribution is not to search for the differences between British English (BE) and American English (AE). Such differences have been established to some extent only and do not suffice to create new, separate languages. BE and AE (and to a certain degree also Canadian and Australian English) are closely related in the same way as parts of their histories and real-life situations. Consequently, it may be problematic and often impossible to define these differences unambiguously.

Sometimes it is difficult to say which word or expression is typically American. Therefore, in spite of the fact that this contribution adresses the American language and the American way of life and tries to point out the most typical features of its influence on Czech reality, as to the language itself, this paper uses the combined term "English/American language" (EAL). The significance of this influence should also not be ignored with regard to its quantitative expansion as well as to the powerful position and prestige of the American world.

As for the relationship of the Czechs to America and her language, there had been contacts even earlier, mostly due to the Czech immigrants living in the United States. It may be interesting to note that the first English-Czech Dictionary was not published in the Czech lands, but in America, by Charles Jonáš in Racine, a town in the state of Wisconsin, in 1876.

3. America's Impact After 1989
Since the Velvet Revolution in 1989, there has been an enormous increase in the demand for the English/American language in the Czech Republic. Besides the study of English, and particularly of American English, the American influence has been booming also in economy, culture and education, politics, press and mass media, social behavior, and other areas of life.

As said above, before 1989, the Czechs had some contacts with the American world. Many of them believed that world to be the magic country in which both money and career could be achieved miraculously without much effort. Of course, such simplifications and generalizations were largely due to a lack of proper information on the life and culture in America.

After the opening of the borders between East and West, in 1989, these views reinforced and strongly affected people´s attitude towards America and everything. But what is the magic making this impact so strong? Is it the belief in the great American Dream? To many Czechs, America has become an even more magic symbol of the promised land, of human freedom, challenge and endeavor, a hope for the better. At present the Czech lands are undergoing great changes. After half a century of regimentation and dullness of all sorts, they are longing for new ideas and styles - frequently inspired by America - which they are ready to accept.

The extent of adopting the American way of life and thinking, lifestyle and culture depends on various factors:

- It depends on a person's background and life experience, on the level of education, on the social status, on whether someone lives in the city or countryside, and his/her job or age. By their very nature senior citizens are more conservative than the younger generations. There are people, both young and old, who tend to adopt everything that is or appears to be American, and there are others who vehemently reject anything that comes or seems to originate from the New world.

- To some degree adopting or rejecting Americanisms is often a matter of temporary fashion, of the social necessity of differentiation, or of prestige. In it social pressure and doing like the Joneses play an important role. For Czechs to be „in" these days, means to speak

English well, to have contacts with one of the probably most influential countries in this world, to be in and live like the Americans do.

- Par exellence, Americanization has become a question of social individual needs and motivation as well as of further development of the country.

- But whatever the Czechs' attitude towards this takeover, one should keep in mind that America is a highly pragmatic country, and that her Dream - whether it has truly been achieved or remained a myth - could not and will not have been realized by dreaming only.

4. Areas of American Influence
The export of the EAL, of the American views, habits, and way of life, into the Czech Republic covers an unbelievably large spectrum of situations. It is reflected in a large number of mutually interwoven and overlapping areas and fields of Czech life, which to single out is impossible. And all the different areas are closely connected and influence one another. Thus, if we speak, let us say, about the American impact upon our economy, we have to mention, at the same time, economic behavior as well, which in turn is not far from social behavior, civilizational aspects, culture, and everyday life situations.

Among these areas the **Czech language** probably is most typical and powerful for the influence of the U.S. The use of EAL binds and accompanies America's impact upon other human activities and simultaneously penetrates Czech life.

Among these lexical transfers there are words and terms exclusively American. There are also expressions used both in American English (AE) and British English (BE). Moreover, American English makes use of vocabulary from other languages, e.g. from Latin, French, Spanish, German, Dutch, Indian, Italian, and others. Many of these terms have become integral parts of AE and are exported from the US as elements of life in the United States. Consequently, such expressions as *barbecue, chilli, potato* from Spanish, *boss* and *Santa Clause* from Dutch, *noodle* and *seminar* from German, *image* from French, *juke-box* from West-African and *spaghetti* and *pizza* from Italian, have also been included in this investigation.

Due to the new motivation since 1989, the attitude towards learning foreign languages in the Czech Republic has completely changed. After half a century of Russian predominance, English has became the number one language, particularly also to businessmen and the youth. The English language and particularly its US version is associated with success - social or economic, with democracy and freedom, with the ability to communicate with the outside world, with the chance of finding a good job with a foreign firm, with the opportunities of job promotion, of reading newspapers, magazines and technical literature and of travelling to foreign countries.

The transfer of AE and BE vocabulary into Czech has become a significant process.

This process involves a large number of EAL words that were and have been adopted either in their original forms as new words or as parallels to their Czech equivalents. While this process began in the past, its intensification can now really be noticed : Unbelievable numbers of AE and BE words are being adopted by the Czech language with modifications being only slight and of a "cosmetic" character, particulary in the spelling and pronunciation of the loan words. Illustrations might be *toast, management, know-how, E-mail, travel, poster, exit, workaholic, airbag, billboard; product / produkt / výrobek; change / smenárna; company / spole čnost; horor, aerobik, kredit karta, kampus, kontrakt, limuzína,* etc.

In a number of cases, new „Czech" verbs have been derived from EAL lexemes by adding Czech prefixes or suffixes, e.g.
*park**ovat** / to park; **z**abuk**ovat** / to book; limit**ovat** / to limit; **z**afix**ovat** / to fix;* model**ka** */ model; bank**a** / bank,* etc.

The quantity of adopted words and phrases depends on the importance of the area in question. In the past EAL expressions among others mainly penetrated the fields of **science, technology , trade, transport, and sports.** Examples for the lexical borrowing are:

laser, display (also in the Czech spelling *displej), import, export, business* and its Czech form *byznys, kontrakt, bus, transport, motel, basketbal* (in the Czech spelling with one „l") and *surfing.*

At present the usage of AE vocabulary, among others, is largely connected with such booming, most popular activities as **business in general, marketing, management, banking, entrepreneurship, advertising** and the **press.** Some frequently used unchanged or adapted Americanisms are:

barter, joint venture, mass-market consumer, franchising, depozitum, (deposit), bank card, kredit karta (credit card), logo, bonus, profit, debit, change, foreign currency, cash flow, distributor, dumping, company, produkt (product), prezentace (presentation), leasing, broker, dealer, interview, boss, fax, job, shop, E-mail, squawk box, check, catalog, commercial, agency.

culture - especially in the **film industry, television, politics and administration, education, music, eating habits, shopping, social life, clothing and fashion**, e.g:

video, klip (clip), show, story, soap opera, color, cartoon, thriller, science fiction, horror, child line, taboo, skinhead, underground, hobo, lídr (leader), prezident (president), no comment, summit, yuppie, talk show, movie, faculty, teenager, music, mega juke-box hits, Country hitparáda (hit parade) Top Ten, OK, pop, band, Prague Post, hamburger, cheeseburger, hot dog, fast food, pop-corn, cracker, toaster, sauce, drink, steak, French fries, instant soup, toast bread, cups and spoons, orange juice, skim milk, brownie mix, make-up, šortky (shorty), body, T-shirt, modelka (model), Czech Top Model, cotton, facelift, store, second hand, supermarket, hypermarket, chain, sale, teleshopping, scanner, pay cash.

The Czech language has also been enriched by many new expressions in **traveling, the tourist industry, sports activities, body and health care:**

travel, last minute trip, stand-by ticket, business class, charter flight, coach, parking, suites, car rent, airbag, air-conditioner, limuzína (limousine), terminál (terminal), aerobic energy, fitness center, body lotion, baseball, skiing, skateboard, snowboard.

Widely used are BE and AE words in the names of
- **buildings, institutions, stores and restaurants,** e.g.:

Business Club, Union Bank, Night Club, Change, English Language Center, Bookstore, K-mart, Mc Donald's, Jewelry/Jewellery, Dance Club, Real Estate Agency, Warner Brothers Home Video.

- in **competitions, prizes, sports events, tournaments and leagues,** e.g.:

  US Open, Czech Indoor, Fed Cup, ATP Tour, Rally Camel Trophy, World Championship, NBA, NHL, WW Wrestling, WCW Wrestling,

- **firms,** e.g.:

  WOODFACE, spol. s. r. o. CINEMATON, INTERSONIC, TELECOM, TIC, Procter & Gamble Company.

- **product and brand names,** e.g.:
  Vaseline Intensive Care, Kleenex tissues, Estée Lauder Parfum Beautiful, eye make-up remover wipes, speed stick deodorant, deostick, glycerine hand therapy, Secret anti-perspirant, paper towels, hair spray, shampoo, skin perfecting creme, toothpaste, oral mint waxed tape styling gel, Johnson & Johnson cosmetics, potpourri, Philip Morris products, Scotch magic type, correction fluid, Whirlpool dryer, mikrovlnka (micro-wawe), No Frost Freezer, chilli hot beans, fish fillets, Kellog's cornflakes, jellied cranberry sauce, Coca-Cola, Diet Coke, Pepsi-Cola, Peter Pan peanut butter, Jack Daniel's whiskey, Lay's potato chips, Grated Parmesan Cheese, Wrigley's chewing gum, Uncle Ben's, Good Year tires.

- **drugs and vitamins,** e.g.
  Natures Bounty, etc.,

- technical and computer terms, programs, industrial and communicative projects, e.g.:

> *product line, copier, word processor, modem, instruction manual, notebook, Internet, electronic typewriter,* and many others.

There are even some **idioms and phrases** (translated word by word into Czech), e.g.:

be in the red / black, - být v červených/černých číslech.

Abbreviations and letter-words

SAT, IBM, P.O.Box, KFC, AIDS, UFO, WWW, B-B-Q, UPS, DHL, c.v., ATM, VIP, MGM, AT&T, VCR, CNN, Inc., RSVP, are now used very often in manifold fields.

With the EAL demand the interest in EAL teaching and English-American language instructors arose. After 1989, many organizations (Education for Democracy, Peace Corps, religious groups), sent their volunteers to help with teaching, most native speakers coming from the USA. Courses in English, mainly in AE were offered in Advanced conversation, as well as for beginners and false beginners, in English for Special Purposes (ESP), TOEFL, specialist English for managers, banking, secretaries, industry, medicine, the health services, and in many other fields. Practically any English/American native speaker could find a teaching job in the Czech Republic. However, with the improving standard of the EAL knowledge, most institutions are nowadays seeking qualified and experienced teachers.

The use of English, both written and/or spoken, is closely connected with modern American-style **advertising** and the **mass media.**

Advertisements containing AE language can be found practically everywhere: on TV, in the radio, in the newspapers, and magazines; in the middle of movies (on the Nova and Prima TV channels), on billboards, in posters. Some advertisements contain only some English expressions and phrases, some are exclusively in English - mainly those offering good jobs.

Advertisements vary as for their styles and strategies. To attract the customers´ attention the Czech business enterprises spend vast sums of money on advertisements, commercials, TV talk shows, stickers and decals.

There are now money-off discount coupons, free samples of goods in the stores, in-store demonstrators, mail shots and publicity leaflets and window displays, all of them marketing strategies orginally from America.

Similarly, today's Czech language of advertising has been affected by American influence. It is very special, charming, both simple and sophisticated, with short sentences expressing clear purpose. The English expressions used in the advertisements are mostly of an international character, sometimes adjusted to or combined with Czech lexems or supplemented by explanations in Czech. Frequently, the spelling is American. Advertisements are often situational and easy to understand. Some examples are:

AUTOPORT, INSTOP SERVICES, FAMILY FROST, HAIR BOOSTER!, PROFSERVIS, PROFCAR - PRODEJ FSO TRUCK, MASTERCARD - OFFICIAL CARD EURO '96, CAR STYLING, MOTOR TUNING, INFO-KUPON, SEAT CAR COMPLEX s.r.o., NICE´N EASY, TOY STORE, JEANS SPORTSWEAR, TELEMARKET, SKIFUN, LOOX, ULTRA LIGHT, HIGH SCHOOL.

This linguistic infiltration goes hand in hand with the American impact upon all aspects of Czech life.

The political changes of 1989 first of all have heavily impacted on **politics,** the **administration, business** and the **economy;** they have influenced the Czech business culture and economic behavior.

A host of **American consultants, professional advisors and experts** have come to help the country to develop. In hot pursuit of opportunities, **American business owners, entrepreneurs and service providers have** arrived to launch their own businesses and to look for markets. American economic thinking and the sense of business entailed penetrated the Czech entrepreneurial spirit.

A substantial number of American companies have business operations in the Czech Republic. Examples are:

IBM, Microsoft, Procter & Gamble, Johnson & Johnson, FORD, Kaiser Steel, Hayes Wheels, Philip Morris, McDonald's, Pizza Hut, KFC.

According to the estimates, in 1994, the US expatriate population in the Czech Republic soared to about 30,000 (living mostly in the capital). In 1989, there were fewer than 100 Americans in the country.

In the CS **banking system**, many new banks have been established offering more customer services, money transactions, wire transfers. A network of ATMs (automatic telling machines) operating around the clock has been installed nationwide.

Following the American pattern, the Czech Republic now has a **credit card economy.** Credit cards are being used in some parts of the country and people, mainly foreigners, use "plastic money" instead of cash in hotels and stores. Modern ways of making payments are by VISA, MasterCard, American Express, and traveler's checks.

As in America, in the CR **communication and business contacts** with the outside world are facilitated by computers, fax, answering machines, E-mail, mobile phones and speaker phones. A range of telecommunication services wider than ever before is being offered (comprehensive Yellow (Golden) Pages, calling cards, highly efficient telephones, international roaming, etc.). The respective services of American telecommunication companies, e.g. of AT&T, serve as models.

A response to the political and economic changes is the growth of new, unprecedented **job opportunities.** The variety of jobs has changed the attitude towards professional career and work ethic has become a new and different one. Lifetime employment with one firm only is no longer an ideal. As in the American society work carries a high priority. The road to success is associated with hard work, flexibility, efficiency and discipline. Initiative and courage are welcomed, taking any job available rather than being unemployed is preferred. Absences for illnesses or "family emergencies" are not so frequent as before the Revolution of 1989. Such social categories as "workaholics", "yuppies" and „jobless or unemployed people" have emerged. A "résumé" or „CV" (curriculum vitae) no longer is a „family history", but a record of past work experience.

Unlike during the socialist era, people now are much more concerned about their "**image**". The American concept of one's „image" has been imported large scale to the Czech lands by American business and advertising. In the past "a good image" consisted mainly of the type of clothing people wore. Now it also means the care people take of their bodies, the way they speak and behave. It has become fashionable to have a sports club membership, go to a fitcenter, a beauty shop or beauty parlor. In the past few years, in Prague alone about 120 fitcenters were established. To be slim and "in shape" sometimes even constitutes an important qualification when applying for a job. The interest in **exercising, looking after one´s body and health, eating healthy foods**, is the order of today´s fitness craze. Businesses selling ecological cosmetics, beauty drugs, vitamins, plastic surgery, permanent make-up (tatoo), diets, or offering help against anorexia and bulimia, flourish. The **retirement age** has been moved up, the system of health care is changing, many health insurance companies have been set up and have become necessary and useful institutions. A greater concern is now devoted to the **disabled and handicapped people.** Suffering from depression? No worry, as in America, there are now plenty of psychologists and psychiatrists ready to help.

Post-socialist times have brought an array of American-inspired **sports,** step aerobics, joyrobics, jogging, golf, tennis, squash, bowling, racketball, windsurfing, hanggliding, and biking.

America has impacted on the Czech lifestyle. The attitudes to **smoking and alcohol consumption are gradually** changing, so does **lifestyle**. Some people say that the social development in the very heart of Europe resembles the late American 1960s and 1970s, i.e. the explosion of the joy of life and creativity, and **drug addiction**.

In accordance with the capitalist (American) structural pattern of society, the distinctions between **the rich and the poor** have intensified. Current topics for people to speak of are money, profits, commissions, taxes. Their relationship to material possessions has become much closer than ever before. The Czechs now are acquiring what the Americans take for granted: **economic thinking.** Money is everywhere. Today, it plays an important role even in the relationships with family members, friends, and the country.

Life has become faster, hectic and more colorful. Society starts to become **multicultural**. Now, many religions and sects have begun to be active. **Social behavior** is undergoing enormous changes. Crime, violence, group movements and AIDS as well as the protection against it are on the rise and have become daily topics of discussion. Gambling, gambling machines and casinos are „in".

American culture and Czech families and teenagers

Traditional functions of the **family** are transferred out of the home and into the hands of institutions. The Czech parents of today are worried about such deep incisions in family life and in society. The divorce rate is very high. The economic sitution has severely affected even the **man - woman relationship.** More and more women have become career women and have opened their businesses and are economically independent. Many of them shave their legs as American women do. The use of contraceptives has become more widespread than before. A new DINK (Double Income No Children) type of the family has become fashionable and the US sort of speaking of and handling "sexual harassment" gains popularity.

Under the influence of modern American life, Czech parents have come to have much less control of their **children**, and outside forces such as television, schools, and peer group pressures heavily impact on childrens' behavior and attitudes. It is especially the **teenagers** who tend to form gangs and subgroups to share their feelings with their peers. The teenage problems and emotionality necessitated many 'Help Lines' to be established to assist the young.

Czech teenagers are great consumers of American culture. They love to watch American movies. *Beverley Hills 902 10, Melrose Place, Star*

Trek, Baywatch, Bodyguard, Look Who's Talking, Batman, Forever Young, Top Gun, Cliffhanger, Home Alone, and others, are their favorites. They are crazy about American *pop music (Michael Jackson, Madonna, J. Bonjovi, Mariah Carey, Extreme, Guns'n Roses, Whitney Houston,* and many others), *walkmen, compact discmen, discos, Harley Davidsons, roller skating* (with earphones on), *skateboarding, step aerobics, joyrobics, Wrigley's chewing gum, computer games,* and collecting *ice-hockey* and *basketball cards.* Their speech is full of English and American expressions, sometimes even of dirty or obsence ones: hi!, O.K., super, right away, great!, good for you, perfektnì (perfect), love you, absolutely, sure, baby, fuck, and many others. They love *house music,* dancing *rap, step, rock'n roll, break dance, country- line dancing,* and *second hand clothing.* As many adults they often feel comfortable in **American and Western style clothing,** *jeans* with *leather belts, shorts, sweatshirts, cotton T-shirts, baseball caps* with *logos,* and *tennis* and *sports shoes.*

Speaking of the American influence upon the Czech **culture,** one should take into consideration the different backgrounds and the histories of the two nations. Americans feel free from limitation by their history which gave them the freedom of expressing their dreams, feelings and needs. Some of them even deny that there is an "American culture" since Americans frequently are said to prefer material satisfaction to spiritual values and needs.

But despite this claim and although the Czechs', due to their history, have a hierarchy of cultural values different from those of the Americans, the Czech culture, whether we like it or not, is strongly   influenced by America. Some areas of the Czech culture are really becoming Americanized.

Leisure time activities - music and films

The American cultural "invasion" manifests itself mainly in the **pop music and movie industry**. American pop singers are very popular in the Czech Republic and many pop stars come to have their performances there. The Czech people like to listen to jazz, blues, rock, country and western music. Juke-boxes can be found in mainy places. Many American music clips are run in the Czech TV.

Czechs increasingly adopt (American) **television culture** and, as in America, many "couch potatos" like to relax in front of TV screens. It is not only the young people who are crazy about American movies and soap operas, but the adults as well. The Czech TV channels continuously run them, particularly the private TV channels NOVA and PRIMA which show American movie serials and broadcast the latest news in the American pattern with the frequent and typical interruptions for advertising spots and commercials. Even HBO is available and thanks to satellite dishes people can watch American movies on other European TV channels.

Most popular serials are, among others, *Dallas, Dynasty, Falcon Crest, James Bond Junior, M.A.S.H., Hospital Chicago Hope, Moonlighting, The Simpsons, Columbo, Jake and Fatman, Matlock, Tom and Jerry, Walt Disney series*, other cartoons and stories for children, comics, thrillers, horrors, crimes, westerns, science fiction. There are plenty of new Czech programs, and not surprizingly, all the American terminology that goes with them, e.g. shows, quiz-shows, contests (e.g. *Bingo, Carousal, Maxirisk, Carusošou* etc.), talk shows, panel discussions and debates (*V.I.P.*) and other live broadcast, showbusiness and entertainment programs, English language courses (*Family Album*), sports events and sport programs (*Power Play*). Finally, CNN brings the latest news to the Czech viewers in English from all over the world.
Some Czechs feel that the continuous showing of certain film genres touches on the limits of human sensitivity for morals, that sex, crime and

violence are being promoted, and that the people's feelings are exposed to strong pressure.

The Czechs no longer are the movie goers they used to be. Now, they often use video rental services and watch TV at home. And if they do go to the movies, in some cities they may patronize **new types of cinemas,** so-called multicinemas, where several films are shown simultaneously. The American TV and movie industries are very powerful and their commercial spirit has become deeply rooted in the Czech cultural and ethic value system.

Further areas of culture both high and pop that have gained popularity in the Czech Republic are the American **modern arts** (e.g. *graffiti*) and **fiction** (e.g. *Danielle Steel, Ann Rice, Jackie Collins, Ivana Trump*), **romance novels** (e.g. *Harlequin*), and **musicals** (*Jesus Christ Superstar).*

Before 1989, Western publications were forbidden in the socialist republics. After the Velvet Revolution, practically any American **newspaper and magazine** has become available, e.g. *USA Today, Time, Newsweek, Prognosis, The Wall Street Journal, Washington Post, Reader's Digest, National Geographic, Cosmopolitan, Playboy, Hustler.* In the Czech Republic many **catalogs , brochures and literature** (either in Czech or in EAL), e.g. on American life and institutions, travel guides, vocabulary, are offered for sale and provide information on the country and nation across the ocean. All these printed materials exert an influence on the Czech readers.

Educational system

Education usually is more immune against outside influences than other societal domains. Yet, there has been some American influence on the Czech system of **education** in spite of the fact that the American educational system is so different from its European counterparts. Under the American educational influence, now many educators argue that the Czech schools should teach their students to be more independent, self-confident and self-reliant and should be given more freedom.

Similar to American conditions, there is also a current trend with Czech **school children and university students to supplement their pocket money by making a little money on the side.** It is not uncommon for university students to run their own businesses or go abroad to work. From time to time they have a chance of going to the United States to get a temporary job with the Camp America organization, or as an au-pair. In addition, there are **exchange study programs** with American high schools and universities which reinforce multiculturalism, culture shock and cross-cultural learning; popular American topics often spoken of in the Czech Republic.

The **teacher - student relationship** is becoming less formal and more democratic. More types of postgraduate programmes of study are available and many **private schools** have been established. The cost of study is continuously rising. In the universities the **Bachelor degrees** and the **PhD. studies** have increasingly gained importance and recognition.

Even **American-type postgraduate schools**, which prepare for MBA degrees, have been installed in the Czech Republic under such names as *The Czechoslovak Management Center in Celákovice* or *The US Business School in Prague.*

The **Social life** of the Czechs is sometimes enriched by American-style *Valentine's Day and Mother's Day.* This, of course, depends on one's taste. Holiday cards are becoming a big business. Some Czechs, especially the wealthy, organize more and more parties and activities for business or charity purposes.

Travel

Since 1989 **traveling and the tourist industry** have been booming. There are new hotels and accommodation, e.g. the *Holiday Inn in Brno, or the Hilton - Atrium* in Prague. Meanwhile, charter flights stand-by tickets, business class, and the services they describe are taken for granted. Many newly established travel agencies organize travel to all parts of the world, package tours and last minute arrangements have become common.

There is much **traveling by car**, and the Czech streets are nowadays overcrowded with cars of various makes, e.g. American *Fords, Chryslers, Chevrolets, Lincolns, Corvettes, Sunbirds; even pick-ups, jeeps and convertibles* can be seen.

Food and Eating Habits

Usually food and eating habits are considered national attributes and characteristics. They, too, have been subjected to American influence in the Czech Republic. Czechs now patronize fast food restaurants (*Mc Donald's, Kentucky Fried Chicken, and Pizza Hut*) which have gained great popularity. Vending machines can be found everywhere. The Czechs take a liking to finger food and regularly consume **hot dogs, French fries, steaks, instant soups, American salad dressings (Thousand Islands), popcorn, chicken nuggets, sweet dogs, hamburgers, cheeseburgers, pizza, sandwiches, cornflakes, potato chips and sour sauce, Uncle Ben´s** products or **Chilli beans, peanut butter, salsa, tortillas, dorritos, barbecue sauce, tabasco sauce, cantaloupe, chocolate chip cookies, cheese cake, blueberry muffins,** and **banana split,** not to speak of **whiskey, Coca Cola, Diet Coke,**

Sprite, or other drinks of American origin. Nowadays the supermarkets in the CR stock a wide choice of groceries, gourmet foods, seafood, low-fat milk products, hard and soft beverages, frozen foods, instant pre-cooked and pre-packaged dishes, ready-to-eat items and TV-dinners.

Shopping

A genuine proof that American reality has been accepted by and integrated
into the Czech post-socialist shopping culture are **supermarkets**, the American **way of shopping, and stores** (*K-mart, Nike, Levi Strauss*, and other brand stores). Shopping malls and shopping centres are so arranged as to make shopping an entertainment experience à la American, with large-scale displays of an enormous range of goods and services, with bargains and sales, and sometimes even American-type money-back guarantees, with second-hand or used-goods stores, and product recycling programmes all taken care of by crash-course trained „super sales personnel".

Standard of Living

The American Way of Life is also reflected in today´s Czech **standard of the living comfort**. Czech households now sometimes are equipped with washers and clothes dryers, no-frost refrigerators, large deep freezers, dishwashers, coffee-makers, toasters, microwaves, gas and charcoal grills, built-in closets, quilts and patchwork, air conditioners, and other amenities and labour-saving devices. TVs, VCRs, CD players and tape decks and many other electrical appliances, sometimes even computers are quite common. And, speaking of services: There are public laundromats. The first one was the American- run Laundry Kings in Prague, followed by Laundryland, owned and operated by a Czech entrepreneur. Even such luxuries as yachts can be found these days.

People have **pets** again and there are newly passed laws for the prevention of cruelty to animals. **Condominiums, studio apartments and one-family houses** built in an American style can be purchased in the post-socialist lands.

5. Summary

The American influence on the Czechs and their country is often seen as an unavoidable and inevitable accompaniment to the post-socialist Czech political, economic and cultural development. And, indeed, this assumption may be a true one.

This paper examined only the most peculiar and most typical aspects of the American influence on my country. It did not research the influence of other languages and countries upon the Czech Republic, an influence which is also considerable. Sometimes it is very difficult to identify what part of the impact is exclusively American because it very often blends with the development tendencies of the industrialized countries all over the world and, thus, becomes an international influence in the same way as much of the originally American terminology listed here has become global and international. The aspects mentioned in this article were chosen because they are the most conspicuous Americanisms of particular importance.

Not all the areas of the American influence on the Czech Republic after 1989 can be mapped. This impact is of an extraordinary diversity and its degree and depth vary from location to location. In some areas it is very intense, in others it may, however, be almost negligible. But it is ever present, always important, and it should be neither underrated nor overestimated.

America's impact is most intense in the introduction of new ideas, high-tech, specialized know-how, in culture and the entertainment industry. It flourishes most in the cultural and service spheres, particularly also in advertising. It is mainly the consultancy, advisory and advertising firms which play a significant role in the development of the Czech lands. And above all, the English language is seen as essential in linking all these areas with the world, that way making for the changes in progress.

We now live in a democracy and it is up to each of us to decide whether we want our views, culture and our way of life to be Americanized or not.

We can make our choice of accepting or refusing this influence as a whole, or parts of it only. It is our choice whether we want to learn and adopt the American kindness and friendly behavior, self-esteem, proactive attitude, and positive thinking. Perhaps this will be the choice of a chance of looking for one's own cultural awareness and identity and, at the same time, of building a bridge to respect and understanding.

AMERICA IS TOUGH BUT ENGLIGHTENING
Marcela Adámková

„America and Her Influence upon the New Lifestyle of the Czechs". Having spent some time teaching at Southern Illinois University, Carbondale, Illinois, after the collapse of Communism in Eastern Europe, I am now able to compare the lifestyles of Americans and Czechs and present my personal view of the influence America has on our society.

Although there is a wide range of aspects to mention, I would like to concentrate on those topics which are close to me because of my present professional position. Consequently, I would like to comment on such issues as the learning of foreign languages, people's attitude to work, professional success and money, and the position of women in society.

The Czechs have always been the most Westerly of the Slav nations of Europe, but nearly 50 years of their incorporation into the Soviet empire turned them reluctantly towards the East and, as a result, uniformity governed all aspects of everyday life.

Nowadays, Czech lifestyle has dramatically changed as a consequence of the political and economic upheaval that transformed the country after the Velvet Revolution of 1989. The different social groups of the nation reacted to the sudden political freedom with varying degrees of intensity. Economic reform leading to the introduction of a market system has had a dramatic impact on all individuals.

English as a Foreign Language

Numerous factors attesting to these changes can be seen everywhere in the land. In business, banks, factories and other places of work people are busy studying foreign languages. English is the foreign language of the greatest interest to students in the elementary schools and secondary schools and in the universities. Thus, in the academic year 1995/96, over 56 percent of all students chose to study English as a foreign language at VŠB - Technical University of Ostrava. Compared to the Czechs, the Americans have the advantage of speaking English both as their mother tongue and as a globally recognized foreign language. As a result, Americans are frequently reluctant to learn another language, although some of them realize that they are handicapped to some extent by this communicative lack. When, during my stay in the US, teaching American students the Russian language, I asked them: "Why have you decided to study Russian?", students answered: "An immense country is now accessible to us. We should be ready to cross old bridges and build new ones. Knowing how to communicate is a beginning. It's embarrassing to know that English is spoken more by Russians than Russian is spoken by Americans."

For years experts all over the world have been discussing the issue of what to do in order to be successful at work. One of the theories on how to achieve succes is based on so-called "core skills" which we need regardless of what kind of job we have. Possessing "core skills" makes it highly probable that we will succeed at our work and such skills will even help us when changing jobs. And it is not surprising that one of the skills - possibly the most important one - is the ability to communicate properly. This skill includes not only the communication in the mother tongue, but also that in a foreign language. It is the fact which so-called high-fliers realize, indeed.

In a questionnaire on interview techniques the Czech branch of AISEC, the international organization of students of economics and business administration, asked a number of Czech and foreign business enterprises, among them Škoda, Procter & Gamble, Price Waterhouse and others for the characteristics of their applicants profiles. The most important criteria quoted were education and foreign languages with a command of English practically being considered obligatory.

Before 1989, particularly during the years under communism, English was studied for the purpose of reading, the selection of books and magazines allowed under the system; nowadays, the targets of learning English are much more pragmatic. People have been and are studying that language in order to be prepared to do business with foreign partners, to exchange ideas and to be able to communicate effectively when traveling abroad. English has become the lingua franca of modern life.

The Impact of English on the Czech Language

The impact of English, especially of American English, on the Czech language, is evident in many fields. There is a host of English words in Czech newspapers, magazines, reference books, text-books, on product labels and product descriptions without any translation. People have even become accustomed to using them themselves because they believe them to be more exact for communication or because there is no adequate Czech expression yet. Some examples may serve here the purpose of illustration:

●**Economics -**

manager, management, director, marketing assistant, dumping, leasing, holding, public relations, joint venture, portfolio, logo, company, boom, cash and carry, know-how, Eurocheque, Eurocard, Visa, MasterCard,

American Express, Access account, PIN, balance, travellers cheque, broker, blue chip, clearing centre, sales price, cash, debit

- **Informatics and Communications**
  note-book, modem, processor, palmtop, hardware, software
  wordpad, Internet, EuroTel, E-mail, fax
- **Food Industry**
  hot dog, hamburger, cheeseburger, dressing, chips, Kentucky Fried
  Chicken, Mc Drive, Pepsi-light, toast, fast food, cornflakes, Milky
  Way, Froggy Friends, Family Frost
- **Sport**
  stretching, bowling, trekking, jogging, rafting, skateboard, snowboard,
  squash, fitness centre, hattrick
- **Fashion and cosmetics**
  parka, body, top, top model, jeans, lady's collection, set, bodystyling,
  push up, T-shirt, make up, peeling, spray
- **Mass Media, Culture and Education**
  - Names of Newspapers and Magazines:
    Longevity, Pop Life, Profit, EveryDay Prague, Extratip, ForMen
  - TV channels:
    Sky News, Sky Line, Euronews, Cartoon Network
  - Culture:
    underground, pop - art, horror, thriller, comics, star,
    superman, Palmexman, teletext, teleshopping, Novashopping,
    happening
  - Education:
    grant, credit, superlearning
- **Transport**
  airbag, drive - in, drive - out, pick up, air conditioning, airport, free
  zone, parking, last minute, ski bus, bus stop
- **Health service**
  Drop - In Centre, call centre, Garant Hospital, Coldrex
- **Travel Agencies**
  East West, Ideal Tour, Greece Tour, Holiday Tour

- **Names of Business Companies**
  - Central Group, Credit Real, Velvet International, Tower Trading, Eurobuilding Investements
- **Politics**
  - summit, comeback, no comment, bodyguard, meeting.

Some of the words have been modified under the influence of the Czech language with alterations being mostly graphic adjustments. Thus the English „clip" has become the Czech „klip" and, in a similar way, „display" has become displej, „harddisc" - „harddisk", „lobbyism" - „lobování", „single" - „singl", „cockpit" - „kokpit", „showbusiness" - „showbyznys", „leader" - „lídr", „party" - „párty" and many more.

Money, Job and Succes

Another problem area in post-socialist countries is that of money, work and career, typical phenomena that count in America. With the restoration of the principle of private ownership, the relationship the Czechs have to money has changed dramatically during recent years. As a consequence of the market economy people have begun to become money-orientated. In addition some of them have visited the U.S.A. and have changed their opinion about America as "the promised land". They now know that the United States is a wealthy but also tough country where one has to pay for everything; that you will have to pay if you forget to cancel your appointment at the doctor's, that having been fined for speeding will cause a driver's insurance company to charge a higher premium because he will be seen as a higher accident risk. To ordinary people a rising standard of living largely means an increase in the number of things one "must" buy. Many of the „new musts" are not the goods longed for over decades, but services such as medical insurance, day care for children, college tuition for teenagers, which in the past, the Czechs mostly did not have to pay for.

The way people relate to money has been really surprising to the post-socialist Europeans. Before 1989 thinking about how much something was or what could be got for something was considered almost immoral. Now, the well-known Czech newspaper „Mladá fronta dnes" (Voparová, 1996, 6) asks families what they most lacked in the past. From the twenty items on the list, the first five ranks were taken by: money, followed by good health, acceptable housing, a permanent relationship, and mutual understanding between parents and children. As a result of the analysis the Czech psychologist Vera Caponni in the same newspaper recommends that young people, prior to getting married should be interested in how their partners earn their living and how they spend their money.

Another important discovery in the Czech society is that to become rich does not necessarily have to be connected with crime or illegal activities, an association that, for decades, dominated the thinking of law-abiding citizens. Although an increasing number of Americans no longer believe in it. In a 1996 poll 64 percent of interviewees agreed that the American Dream was impossible to achieve for most Americans (Church, 1996, 33). To today's Czechs - this American Dream, the concept of the self-made man, works and appears alive. Being wealthy and successful now is mostly considered to be due to a person's brilliance, intelligence, and ingenuity.

Unemployment in the United States encourages or requires job-hunting. Consequently, people try to be fit and stay healthy. Protagonists in American movies used to smoke and drink a lot. But in real life, smoking is a danger to a person's health. It means to pay more for doctor's bills, to reduce job promotion, opportunitis, and, finally, to lose money. Yet, in the past such factors were of much less concern to the workers of socialist societies. Under the influence of the Western or, say, American way of life the Czechs have been changing their attitudes to health care and work opportunities. The momentum of this change and its degree may be the same as elsewhere. But the key factor is that jobs - to which the Czech people had a legal claim until a few years ago - have now become very important and significantly influence the nation's style and quality of life. In 1996 the unemployment rate in the Czech Republic (3 percent) was lower than in the United States (5 percent). It is not surprising since privatisation has not yet been completed in the Czech Republic. As a result there is still some of the "artificial" employment in some sectors of the economy. This means that there are more work opportunities than economically necessary.

The Czech unemployment support policy slightly differs from the American one. The U.S. government rather supports active unemployment measures, e.g. training or retraining labour which enable people to work in new and different fields. Unemployed people are helped only temporarily in order to be able to help themselves later. The Czech government, on the other hand, appears to be keen making unemployed more comfortable, thus, paralysing the individual's efforts to try to find a new job. But, this attitude is changing under the free market system.

Undoubtedly, getting a better job in the U.S. depends on a good education, and that education will have to be paid for. Many American students hold part-time jobs while they are studying. If they do not have the necessary money, the bank might lend it to them, and, after graduation, they will have to repay the loan. Nowadays, an increasing number of Czech students both study and have part-time jobs as well. And, following their American role models, they wish to be more independent of their parents, they might want to buy a flat or a car or travel abroad.

The Position of Women in Society

The impact of America on the post-socialist Czech Republic has also changed the role of women in society. As a result of the longer tradition of democracy in the U.S.A., American women when compared to Czech ones seem to be more independent. After 1989, the Western values of equality, individual freedom and equal opportunities were enthusiastically wellcomed by the Czech people. Many women realized the new opportunities in their lives and began to become career-minded. Now, they run businesses, have interesting jobs, earn more money, and have greater and more opportunities to travel. Many of them no longer want to lose their independence just gained and, therefore, do not marry and do not have children before the age of thirty. The demographic behavior changes because young couples postpone having a family. Instead they prefer to build their professional career first and then have children, an attitude which has almost been the norm for people in Western societies.

This development has both positive and negative aspects. Among the positive ones there is a better financial situation for the family, which promotes its prosperity and, undoubtedly, is favourable for the upbringing and education of children. On the other hand, it is rather difficult for professionally successful women to leave their jobs temporarily in order to have and rear a child. Increasingly, young women are faced with the problem of either to be professionally engaged or to have children.

For the issue of professional career versus family life, there are four basic examples of the relationship between wife and husband. They have existed both in Czech and American societies, but to different extents.

The first example is that of the family in which the wife does not work. While in American society this situation has been typical for the middle and higher income families, in the Czech society this family pattern began to reappear after 1989. Prior to World War II it had been quite common in Czechoslovakia, except in lower income families. The husband is often a successful entrepreneur and able to provide for the prosperity of the family. As a rule, the wife is a fulltime housewife looking after the children and a house usually located at the outskirts of the city or in a village near the city. Family life appears to be harmonious, with children having a privileged position. But there are also negative aspects: the husband is often out of the house and feels overworked. Frequently, the husband also cannot cope with such new phenomena as rapid career development, promotion, and high income. The new way of life sometimes makes him change his wife in a similar way as he changes his suit or car. This has a devastating effect on the children. Often the wife begins to suffer from an inferiority complex since contemporary society underestimates and underrates domestic work. She is at home all the time and „only" concentrates on her family. Postsocialist societies have inherited what Americans call "the green - window syndrome": suburban family life with an ever busy and absent husband.

The second example is that of the family in which the wife has given up employment for some time. The wife had a job, but after childbirth she stayed at home. Originally, she had set her mind to a career but, for the benefit of her family, she gave up most of her plans. She wishes to return to work later. Finding part-time work is difficult and, sometimes, she worries because she knows that it will not be easy for her to return to her professional career after the children have grown up.

The third family pattern is the one in which both the husband and the wife are working. One of the partners - usually the husband - devotes more time to his professional career than to family matters The wife usually works from 7.00 a.m. to 3.30 p.m. and then looks after the children, the flat, or the house. Her income is important to family but it is not crucial. Since the husband tries to share in household duties as well, the wife usually finds the situation satisfactory. From the 1950s until our days, family types 2 and 3 have been very common in the Czech society.

A fourth example of the family is the one in which both the husband and the wife are fully engaged in professional careers. The number of such families has increased in the Czech Republic since 1989. Sometimes tension arises within this family relationship if there is no division of work at home. The wife feels overworked which can become a source of conflict. Sometimes families try to tackle the problem by hiring domestic help. But there may be another problem as well. A wife's successful career can affect the husband's role and position. It may be frustrating for a man to accustom himself to his wife's briefcase with a notebook, a mobile phone, a new (business) car and frequent business trips. Psychiatrist František Hájek (Maraculasová, 1994, 10) of a pre-marital advisory centre says that the worst type of a woman for a contemporary man is "a dominating, emancipated and ambitious intellectual". Since success in society is often evaluated and valued in terms of professional careers the self-confidence of such a husband may be reduced. It is no surprise that such families often have only one child who is looked after by its grandparents, or no child at all.

This „Americanization" of family philosophy and life may be one of the reasons why the Czech Republic is one of the European countries which have a falling birthrate. Compared to 1995, in 1996 the birthrate decreased by 4,500. In fact, 1996 was the year with the lowest birthrate in the past two centuries. According to the Czech Office of Statistics it was one of the lowest in the world (Mladá fronta Dnes 1. Jan 1997, 3).

As to the changing role of women in Czech society after 1989, there is another issue which is beginning to be discussed in public as a consequence of the influence and impact of American values and culture.

It is an old and, at the same time, a new matter. It is the problem of sexual harassment which has existed for ages that is now being spoken of publicly as something new.

When being a teacher at Southern Illinois University at Carbondale a couple of years ago, I was asked to sign, besides others, a document forbiding any form of sexual harassment at the university. The document explained what sexual harassment was. It was defined as any unwelcome sexual advances, requests for sexual favours and other verbal or physical conduct of a sexual nature. Sexual harassment can occur within and beyond the classroom and workplace. Harassers are usually male and most victims are female, but persons of either sex may be victims of harassers. Harassment involves a member of the opposite sex, but can also involve two persons of the same sex. It is important to create and maintain a community in which students, teachers and staff can work together in an atmosphere free from all forms of exploitation. Academic freedom can exist only when all persons are free to pursue ideas in a non-threatening, non-coercive atmosphere of mutual respect. Sexual harass-ment runs counter the objectives of the university.

In the U.S.A. sexual harassment, e.g. harassment on the basis of religion and race, is considered to be a form of discrimination and is prohibited by law. It is the violation of Title VII of the Federal 1964 Civil Rights Act.

Some historians (Mehler/ Mrkoš, 1994, 175) say that the American model of success is based on the three principles of freedom, personal prosperity and peace. If political and personal freedom is a starting point for prosperity and peace, the necessity of the liquidation of the discrimination mentioned above is evident both for western and post-socialist countries. Obviously, American influence has led to the fact that such discrimination is now being discussed also in the post-socialist Czech Republic.

Conclusions

Summing up, things have been changing drastically in the Czech Republic. Yet, it appears quite normal that people react differently to the changes during what still is a transitional and volatile period. There are optimists and pessimists who see the future development from different perspectives. To some extent it depends on how strong and self-assertive people are when carrying out their plans. Some time ago, I overheard an analogy in which the people's feelings in post-socialist countries were compared to the ones of animals from a zoo which were given freedom. Some of the animals were happy to be able to leave their cages and make use of their much-desired freedom. But other animals, which found out that nobody looked after them, decided to return to the "safety" of their cages. Life there was restricted, but it provided some kind of security. This analogy, to some extent, corresponds to the situation in my country.

Is the American influence really tough, and is it really enlightening?

Hopefully, the Czech government will be wise and strong enough to safeguard peace and personal prosperity for the people living in the Czech Republic, and, at the same time, ensure the transfer of the positive experience of the Western, i.e. also American civilization to the life of the Czechs. May that government and the Czech people also be wise enough to eliminate from that influence the negative and unwanted effects. If we are really successful, the Czech American experience will, indeed, have been tough but enlightening.

49

Literature:

Voparová M. (1996) : Peníze až na prvním míste, Mladá fronta Dnes,
Víkend, October 26, p. 6
Church G. J. (1996): Are They Living Better?, Time, February 5, 1996,
p. 33
Maraculasová E. (1994) : V manželství by nikdo nemel usilovat o
prvenství, Zdravotnické noviny, November 25, p. 10
V zemi se opět narodilo méně dětí, Mladá fronta Dnes, January 1, 1997
Mehler Ha. A., Mrkoš B. J. (1994): Umení vládnout, Melantrich, p.175

AMERICAN CULTURE IN ESTONIA
Mari Uibo

In the Soviet school of semiotics, differences in cultures were perceived as a positive feature, a source of development. Whatever culture we speak about, be it the culture of a nation, of a small community, a group of people who have temporarily come together, or the culture of a separate individual, it is the differences that make a difference. Through our differences we contribute to the diversity of the world.

Over the centuries, Estonia has managed to preserve a distinctly original culture. It has been influenced by the Danes, the Swedes, the Germans and the Russians, but the language and the core of the culture have remained. Traditionally, Estonians are considered to be reserved, conservative, unemotional and stubborn. The latter feature is supposed to account for the failure of the different invaders to break the spirit of the people. Subjectively, I would define Estonians as a proud nation with the intelligence of the woods, respect for education and contempt for violence.

Estonia, the Way It Used to Be
As most people probably do not know what and where Estonia is even at this time, let me say a few words about her background to at least try to justify my pride in being an Estonian.

Illiteracy was done away with in Estonia by the turn of the century. By 1895, 95 percent of the population could write and read and all the adult population were literate because, after the Reformation, pastors would not wed couples who could not read. During the more than 700 years of foreign occupation, education was not encouraged since it was considered dangerous; but, it was not totally suppressed.

Books by Estonian authors have been translated into many languages and all the world classics have been translated into Estionan.

As to Estonian contempt for violence, here are a few examples:

My mother tells me that when the Russians took over in 1940, Estonian men started to disappear. Uniformed men came for them under the cover of the night and took them away. They never came back. Then, in the summer of 1941, rumours spread that they had been conscripted into the Soviet Army and were being taken away to the front by warships. The women and children hurried to the harbour. They were late. The ships were about to sail. Some women began swimming towards the ships. The Russians opened fire. There was nothing left but to sing. The women sang a song on the shore and the men answered with another song from aboard the ships. That was their only farewell. Many of the men never returned....

Another example. In 1990, when Soviet Estonia had declared its transition to independence and had the first popularly elected Estonian government, the Russian hardliners tried to take over the seat of the government in Toompea Castle. It was a situation fraught with complications. Although they had not managed to overthrow the government, they could have provoked violence, which would have been very welcome, because then the Russian tanks would have had a pretext to enter the capital in order to „protect the Russian minority" (about 50 percent of the population of the capital at the time!). The prime minister came on the air to ask people for help. His message came in the middle of an entertainment programme of music and jokes. At first, we thought that it was another joke but, after repeated calls for help we knew that the situation was serious. I had an evening class half an hour later, so I waited and we went to town all together. By then everything was over. People had come from all over Estonia armed with rakes and spades. Following the instructions of the well-known and respected actor and stage-director Mikk Mikiver, they did not use their 'weapons'. They split into two files, forming a narrow passage for the hardliners to leave through and started to sing Estonian national songs with the shouts „Out!" in between. The only case of violence was the Russian hardliner who was crushed against the gates by his companions from behind when they were trying to break through into the castle.

In 1988, when Estonia was in the midst of the Singing Revolution, I was acting as an interpreter at an important international exhibition. One of its organisers was acting as a 45 year-old American who had just undergone a cancer operation. He went to one of the singing protest events against the Soviet rule in Song Festival Grounds. He said he had never been so moved in his life or felt such powerful a passive resistance.

Estonia Today

Today we are arming ourselves. We want to join NATO. Fortunately, we are not yet as militant as the Lithuanians, who have opened a bar called NATO in Vilnius. In addition to a display of guns, grenades and mock missiles, it has a menu offerning „Red Mine Caviar", „Demarcation Chicken" and „Remains of a Partisan".

I think the threat of losing our identity has never been so strong, even if people light-heartedly speak about the fear of Americanization. One of the reasons may be that all the past influences were coercive and came from cultures that were considered inferior by the arrogant Estonias, who always preferred to keep themselves to themselves rather than 'sell their souls to the Evil One'.

McDonaldization has reached Estonia, both physically and morally. There are three McDonald's in Tallinn and now we are seriously talking about better ways to sell ourselves.

Education

We speak the language of standardization, efficiency, calculability, and profit even in education. The rector of one of the biggest Estonian universities earnestly compared the university to a hairdresser's salon. We, at the university, all sell services and have to find the best ways to satisfy the customer. What he overlooks is the difference in responsibility. If somebody makes a mess of my hair for the sake of fashion, let's say, or for the sake of charging extra money for a fancy hairdo, I may suffer for a month or two. Other people may notice it or not, but even that will not make much of a difference. If, however, somebody makes a mess of my education, the whole society may suffer irreparable losses. Of course, the rector's simile was metaphorical, but the language we use reflects the changes in our mindset. In the long run, the shift from humanistic/ethical to managerial/entrepreneurial approaches to education may result in a dehumanization of the whole of mankind.

Pop Culture

Pop culture, they say, has turned to the West with a vengeance (forbidden fruit in the past!). Radios play mostly Western pop music. Some local bands now sing only in English. TV stations are full of action films and soap operas from the United States; commercials interrupt good films every ten minutes.

The other day I could not watch a French comedy on TV, because my daughter and her boyfriend wanted to watch a Quentin Tarantino film. It was „The Reservoir Dogs". After the first scene soaked in blood, I locked myself in my room so as not to hear the shouting.

My sister, who does not have a room of her own, said she left for a walk, because her 15-year-old son had insisted on watching the film. On the next day, he came for a visit and started talking about the film. He seemed to have been most impressed by the torture scene in which somebody had his ear cut off. He went on and on about it till I was sick. He said he would have cut off the guy's nose. He was joking of course, but then ... He is quite a tough little chap already. I do hope he will grow out of it.

With all due respect to the genius of Quentin Tarantino, I think he can be dangerous, especially for unprepared minds. I went to see „Pulp Fiction" which is a sophisticated film, very much tongue in the cheek. The movie theatre was full of teenagers who laughed in all the wrong places, I am afraid.

Language

Speaking of the language, I am happy to say that in „Pulp Fiction" it took quite some Estonian words to translate the meagre all-embracing obscenities of the film dialogues in the subtitles. In everyday life, teenagers mostly use English dirty language. It is crowding out the Russian obscenities that were used mainly in the Soviet Army and were reserved to certain low-class registers. The English language being so much more foreign, probably makes dirty language psychologically more acceptable and pop at the same time. Sorry, I mean, „cool".

In Estonian young people's slang, about 20 percent of the words are of English origin. They play around with words like 'kissima' - to kiss, 'mani' - money, 'sliip' - sleep, 'pleiss' - place (meaning a vacant place where one can have a party, often involving sex), 'drinkima' - to drink alcohol with no excess, etc. In computer jargon, the percentage of English words is even higher, which, I think, is fair since computers originated in America.

What is worrying me is that the Estonian everyday language is becoming more and more polluted with Americanisms. A Ministry of Education official said that his son, coming home from school, was unable to utter a single purely Estonian sentence. Every other word was English or distorted English. In a conversation with a Theatre Institute graduate, some time ago, I heard, for example, „Selles ongi asja point". Translated from Estonian it would mean „That is the point of the matter" which sounds as redundant in Estonian as it does in English. I, myself, have been reprimanded by an Estonian friend for using 'OK' and 'sorry' instead of the Estonian words which are as simple. Somebody said that the universal language of the 21st century will be a distorted English of some kind. Older people are aware of the danger, but I am not sure they will have enough authority to stop the process. The young people will say that the older generation are just splitting hairs.

Social Behavoir
Politics

In politics there is a perceptible shift towards Americanization. This is hardly surprising since the United States have a much older history of democracy than many other countries in the world. The clumsy attempts to adopt the American model has resulted in electoral procedures that are far from flattering to the Estonian state. The last presidential elections (1996) were classified very bad theatre by many observers. Mud slinging has come into fashion in the media as a weapon in political games. Respect for privacy and decent attitudes that we used to take pride in are rapidly disappearing.

I think that one of the reasons why Estonians cannot cope with the idea of a democratic government might be that, in Hofstede's terms, Estonia has, out of necessity, always been a land remote from large-power countries. Consequently, power and authority of position have always been associated with corruption. So, people who have a natural ability for leadership keep away from politics and leave it in the hands of those who are not always best qualified or ethically suitable for the job.

The Cult of Money

Making money is very important and 'to have' is increasingly becoming equated with 'to be'. The percentage of people for whom money is the most important thing in life is still fairly small, but people feel the pressure of having to make money very strongly. Those who are not used to the idea of selling themselves feel alienated, and the suicide rate increased by 30 percent during the first few years of independence (612 in 1994 compared to 425 in 1990). The drinking problem as part of overall escapism has always been there; it is now aggravated by drugs.

This is also connected with the commercialised view of the individual. As part of the Professional English course that I teach to my Estonian post-graduate students, I have used some models of professional writing collected by an American colleague. In his collection of successful 'looking-for-a-job' applications, there were a few that used to shock my students as being too boastful and out of place in Estonia. This year, nobody noticed anything strange about them. I have only been using those materials for three years!

With the collectivist set up of society and the past, where 'all were for one' and 'one was for all', being replaced by a highly individualist set up, people lose their sense of security and purpose.

Manners and Morals

We used to have some in the past. Now they are called age and sex discrimination. Young people being seated happily on crowded public transport while old ladies and the handicapped have to stand, is a common sight today. This would have been unthinkable in the past. Some little old lady or dignified gentleman would have told them off. Now nobody dares!

After a few years of Estonian independence, a friend in England told me that the feminist movement would soon reach Estonia. I said there was no danger at all since we had it already. Actually, my great aunt Mari Reiman, whom I was named after, was the founder of the feminist movement in Estonia. She also started the first Estonian feminist magazine at the turn of the century. I thought that now we were back to normal. We want men to be men and women to be women. The more so as in the Estonian language there is no gender distinction and, consequently, no inherent need to fight about it and oppose one gender to the other.

When I returned to Estonia, I noticed that things had changed again. The feminist movement was „in". Men of my generation are shocked when I grab my coat and put it on without the assistance which in the earlier days, was commonly considered a sign of galantry towards a woman. My English or American friends would never dream of showing a woman that she is a lady for fear of being called sexist. Today, not many young Estonians will help a woman into her coat unless expressly asked to do so, nor will some of them not let a woman or an older person pass through the door first either.

At the same time, an English friend told me he found it strange that people in Estonia do not say „thank you", if you hold the door for others or let them pass first. Most of the time I would not do so either, People just find such behavior so natural. But I think it is nice to say „thank you" and „sorry" as a sign to appreciaton to the other people around us. So we too.

Keep Smiling

We have already learned to smile. A few years ago, the Estonian TV producer, Merike Veskus, was surprised to see people smile all the time when she visited the United States for the first time. She asked an Estonian expatriate whether everybody in America was supposed to smile. He said „yes", just in case because you never know whom you are looking at. They may have a gun or a knife and you never know how that knife is going to be used if they do not like your face. So you better not irritate them by not smiling. Now, there are smiles all over in Estonia. Merike says she would prefer a sincere broad smile once in a while rather than see the forced smiles all the time. I, personally, am not sure whether I object to smiling. A smile is the shortest distance between two people and even if it does not cost anything it is valuable as long as it is not a fake.

America Is Not Just McDonald's and Keep Smiling

Whatever negative influences I have pointed out, as a young actor-businessman said to me some time ago , America is not only McDonald's and keep smiling. There is a lot for us to learn. There is quality, optimism, enterprise, creativity, scope, a serious attitude to work and great respect for basic human values. Many good things from America have permeated Estonian culture.

The United States have had an enormous positive influence on the entire world. Just think where we would be without computers, great American films, literature, philosophy, psychology or the managerial sciences? That is probably one reason why the values promoted by mass communication have been so uncritically accepted as true and worthwhile.

Cultural exchange between countries is a most natural and beneficial phenomenon as long as there is no unthinking plagiarism. There is always something good we can learn from other nations. The problem is that Estonia is tiny and America is gigantic. Proportionally, there are probably fewer bad elements in American culture than there are in Estonian culture. But in literal terms, compared to the size of the country and the population, the negative influences can be smothering. Especially, as none of us is completely immune to the American Dream and the perfect world of Disney as the American vision of paradise.

Literature:

Bridge, Adrian (1996): „Frank Zappa and a Bar Called NATO" City Paper (The Baltic States), No. 24, Tallinn, Baltic Office House

Hofstede, Geert, (1983): „Dimensions of National Cultures in Fifty Countries and Three Regions". J. Deregowsky, S. Dziurawiec, and R.C. Annis (eds.): Expiscations in Cross-Cultural Psychology. Swets and Zeitlinger, Lisse, Netherlands

Paluoja, Ene (1996): Usutlus. Teleleht, No. 47. Tallinn. Telekavade Kirjastus. AS Parimenta

Lotman, Ju.M. (1992): Fenomen kultury. Izbrannye statji. Tom I. Statji po semiotike I tipologii kultury (The Phenomenon of Culture. Selected Articles. Vol. I. Articles on Semiotics and Typology of Culture). Tallinn: Alexandra

Foucault, Michel (1988): Politics, Philosophy, Culture. Routlege, Chapman & Hall, Inc. USA

Tarm, Mihkel (1995): Losing My Russian. City Paper (The Baltic States), No.19. Tallinn. Baltic Office House

Landsberg, Mitchell (1995): Anything But A Small Small World. City Paper (The Baltic States), No. 19. Tallinn. Baltic Office House

English Computing Terms in the Slovak Language
Viera Nemčoková

It is very easy to answer the question of what characterizes the second half of this century. Computers! Computers have made their way into all areas of human activity. This fact is particularly reflected in the wide use of computers terminology in various professional groups.

In our brief contribution to this volume we would like to concentrate on the present situation of the use of English technical computing terms in the Slovak language, both in the standard Slovak terminological system and in the professional slang of computer experts.

This use of foreign language register as an integral part of the Slovak language is, of course, a direct result of the political and economic changes of 1989 and reflects the deep-teaching linguistic, social, and cultural impact America has made upon post-socialist Slovakia.

Present situation
After 1989, we have been dealing with computing literature of different qualities, technical norms, officially published professional literature and as we call them, non-official publications, translations of manuals, papers for internal company and institutional use.

The linguistic material analysed here comprises 1,500 lexical items excerpted from computing norms and official professional literature as well as a collection of special expressions from various manuals and technical professional slang.

The analysis of the material indicated shows that the Slovak terminological computing systems comprise only few English computing terms. However, Slovak professional slang is crowded with English terms, although there are adequate Slovak equivalents for the majority of the English professional computing terms.

Standard terminology

As said above the Slovak computing terminological system contains only relatively few technical terms borrowed fom English, e.g. **bit, byte, spooling, packet, PASCAL, BASIC**. In the Slovak language **bit** keeps English spelling and pronunciation. This is also the case with **byte** and **spooling**. While the original spelling of the term **packet** is preserved, the pronunciation is Slovak [paket]. The situation changes slightly in the use of the term **port**. Its spelling is the same both in the Slovak and English languages, but the Slovak pronunciation is based on its written form [port]. The term **start** has its origin in English, yet the speakers of Slovak do not realise its foreign origin. Similarly, English acronyms such as **PASCAL, BASIC**, and others, have become part of our terminological system of computing.

The English bororrowings have been interpolated into the Slovak paradigmatic system and are used in the standard language as well as in the professional technical slang.

Professional slang

Slovak professional slang presents a much more colorful picture of the English and/or American linguistic interference in the field of computing. A comparison of the vocabulary used in this professional slang and in the standard language shows that this professional slang is rich in English computing terms, despite the fact that adequate Slovak equivalent expressions are available for most of the English loanwords.

This phenomenon may be explained from the linguistic and sociolinguistic point of view. Under the linguistic approach, the transfer of lexical items from one language to the other may be achieved in two ways:

1. a lexical unit preserves its original phonetic, phonological and morphological form, i.e. it is not assimilated or changed;
2. a lexical unit is assimilated = its phonetic, phonological and morphological forms are adjusted so as to conform to the conditions of the target language (Stefánik, 1994).

Verbs

Verbs are quite rare in the official Slovak computing terminology. This may be due to a strong tendency to use exact expressions, e.g. a predominance of nouns (Horecký - Buzássová - Bosák, 1989, 254; Mistrík, 1977, 284). The situation is much different in professional slang.

A considerable number of professional terms consist of verbs borrowed from the English terminology of computing. All verbs analysed prove to be hybrids consisting of an English word base plus Slovak suffix. In the process of borrowing, various languages use specific suffixes typical for the given language. Thus, the suffix -„ova" added to foreign verbs is characteristic of the Slovak language. Some examples may illustrate this:

talk - ovat'	→	[talkovat']
escape - ovat'	→	[iskejpovat']
scan - ovat'	→	[sken - ovat']
exit - ovat'	→	[egzitovat']
e-mail - ovat'	→	[imailovat']
boot - ovat'	→	[bu:tovat']
reset - ovat'	→	[resetovat']
zip - ovat'	→	[zipovat']

The word - forming suffix **ova**t is very productive in the word-formative-type noun - ovat: form(a) - ovat, rat(a) - ovat, knih(a) - ovat. Here, the role of analogy employed in the process of assimilation is significant.

Likewise, a few verbs formed by means of the verb-forming suffix **-nút** can be found among the professional expressions:

stop - nút'	[stopnút']
click - nút' / kliknút'	[kliknút']
zip - nút'	[zipnút']

All these verbs express aspect. Those carrying the suffix -ovat are imperfective verbs, those having the suffix - nút are perfective verbs.
The verb zipovat deserves special attention. It forms an aspect pair:

zip - ovat'	imperfectivity
zip - nút'	perfectivity

The verb zipovat itself acts as a word-base for forming new words by prefixation. The word-formative structure of the verbs rozzipovat, zazipovat is: Slovak prefix + hybrid-word base. The meaning of the verb rozzipovat is "to reduce the density of data". The prefix **roz** - means „to put something into an inadequate situation". It gives the verb the opposite meaning. The prefix **za** - emphasises the fundamental meaning; the meaning of **za** - is „to do something very well", "to bring something to perfection", i.e."to add some additional information".

zipovat'	za - zipovat'
roz - zipovat'	

Technical slang comprises a number of professional expressions. The verbs are hybrids. The word-formation is a means of assimilating one type (verbs) of English computing terms to the Slovak language. It is accompanied by changes in pronunciation and spelling. The borrowing of verbs is typical for technical slang.

Nouns

The second dominant group of English professional expressions borrowed is nouns. They are borrowings from the English computing terminology. Some examples are:

software / softvér	[softve:r]
hardware /hárdver	[ha:rdver]
driver / drajver	[drajver]
cartridge/ kártridž	[ka:rtridž]
display / displej	[displei]
bus	[bus]
output	[autput]
input	[input]
buffer / bafer	[bafer]
file / fajl / fajly	[fajl]
help	[help]
listing	[listing]
boot	[bu:t]
scanner / skener	[skener]

From these examples it seems that the original English form and spelling are preserved. In fact, however, the spelling varies between English and Slovak in many cases (software / softvér; driver / drajver). Pronunciation is strictly Slovak. All these loan nouns are treated as inanimate masculine nouns and are assigned to the suitable masculine declension paradigm. The classification criteria are the same as applied to the classification of domestic substantives; the consonant ending is based on the spelling or pronunciation of the particular word.

The substantives ending in a hard consonant (based on spelling or pronunciation) belong to the hard paradigm represented by the paradigm word **dub**: **software, bus, input, output, boot**.

The terms **cartridge** and **display,** having a soft ending (based on pronunciation), are added to the paradigm **stroj** which is the soft paradigm. Both paradigms are masculine.

Some of these substantives serve as a word-base and the words derived from them are adjectives:

software	softwar-ový
desk-top	desktop-ový

Conclusions

Compared to the standard Slovak language, the professional slang of computer experts comprises a large number of English terms which are shorter and more flexible than their Slovak equivalents. The combination of Slovak and English lexemes results in the two most common types of denomiations:

a) hybrid complex naming units:
   e.g. drivery mechaniky, softwarové vybavenie, display počítača, and
b) hybrid word-combinations:
   softwarové prostriedky pre windows; nájdite si to v helpe; chyba je v boote; rýchlost prístupu na hárd disk.

Literature:

Horecký, J.- Buzássová, K.- Bosák, J. (1989) : Dynamika slovnej zásoby súčasnej slovenčiny. Bratislava, Veda, 254

Mistrík, J.: (1977): Stylistika slovenského jazyka. Bratislava, Slovenské pedagogické nakladateľstvo, 284

Stefánik, J.: (1994): Billingvizmus na pozadí dvoch morfologicky odlišných jazykov. Jazykovedný časopis, 45, 111 - 127

ENGLISH AS A FOREIGN LANGUAGE IN POST-SOCIALIST SLOVAKIA
SOME FIRST OBSERVATIONS
Gabriela Knutová

I. Introduction

The political development in Eastern Europe during the past few years has resulted in changes of the social and economic conditions in Slovakia which initiated new directions in many societal domains. These changes had also a considerable effect on the teaching of foreign languages in Slovakia. The purpose of this paper is to analyze and map major trends in this foreign language education.

II. Historical Background

The Slovak system of teaching foreign languages began to change rapidly after 1989. Russian which had been the foreign language Number 1 for over four decades, disappeared almost completely from the schools in the course of a few months. Why did the teaching of Russian collapse totally, not only in Slovakia but also in the other satellite countries of the former East Bloc? Were the causes only political or were economic factors involved as well? And why did English immediately become the widest spread foreign language in Slovakia?

The questions concerning the collapse of the teaching of Russian and the factors determining the selection of specific foreign languages, i.e. English in our case, are interrelated. Before analyzing these factors it is necessary to give a brief review of recent history of the teaching of foreign languages in Slovakia. It appears also worth mentioning that Slovakia has a long tradition of teaching and learning modern foreign languages. In the 1920s and the time thereafter, German was the most-taught foreign language in the country with English and French ranking second.

This can be seen from the curricula of secondary schools in 1934, e.g. the „reálne gymnázium" (grammar or high school orientated primarily towards the sciences) where German was taught for a relatively large number of hours weekly, while English and French were allotted fewer hours.

After World War II, the educational system in Slovakia was restructured. From 1953 on, the teaching of Western foreign languages was considerably limited to two hours per week for three years only. Due to later changes and restructuring in education, the marginal position of Western foreign languages was improved to a more important role reflected in a higher number of teaching hours and the option of having them included in state leaving examinations from 1965 on.

In the late 1940s, Russian was introduced into Slovak education and also into that of other former East-Bloc states. It was a compulsory language in all schools over 10 years, including those of the tertiary sector. Although they had a long tradition in the Czechoslovakian system, the status of other foreign languages (German, English, French) was lowered.

III. Causes of the changes
The long tradition of teaching Western foreign languages in Slovakia has been only one of the factors in the country's foreign language policy. Other aspects also contributed to the spreading of a foreign language and played decisive roles in determining foreign language policy .

The sudden changes, e.g. the reorientation of that policy and a different emphasis on the languages of the West after 1989, are viewed by some people, mainly by former teachers of Russian, as a purely political issue. They blame the Ministry of Education for a lack of support for teaching Russian.

In an article on the present situation of the teaching of Russian in Slovakia, this is clearly expressed by Mikluš (l993, 61). At the same time this criticizm shows that the past 40 years of the history of Slovakia and other former socialist countries provides a good example of how language policy could be strictly determined mainly by the political orientation of the country leaving out of consideration economic or other implications. There are numerous examples in history showing that the spreading of a language is usually closely related to the political and economic impact of the most powerful countries in the world. "Economically strong countries or dynasties could expand not only their political and economic power over new areas, but also in their territories, and with this a spreading of the language over new areas could be noticed, e.g. in ancient Greece the so-called Koine, a special form of ancient Greek, was used by shipping traders in the Mediterranean ports or, under the ecomonic power of the Roman empire, Latin was spread all over the Mediterranean coast and far into Central and Western Europe, or the Norman conquerors who " franchised " the Anglo-Saxon and more recently British colonialism, and the economic expansion of the USA " (Pfeil,1993, 311).

These examples from history may answer the question of why the teaching of Russian practically vanished after the 1989 Revolution. Very likely the most decisive reason was the fact that teaching and learning of Russian were imposed on the educational systems of the Soviet Satellite states. In other words the introduction of Russian into the educational systems was not the result of the natural impact of the political and economic power of the former USSR. According to Northover (1993, 3OO) "Russian was never a world language of trade, or science, and too valuable to be displaced. Nevertheless, if the world language introduced into Slovakia is mastered only by a small political, social and scientific elite, then there is a possibility that they may form values and norms divorced from the attitudes and aspirations of the majority in the country". This might explain why Russian as a foreign language, when no longer supported officially by government, began to disappear without protest from many secondary schools and the universities.

When Russian lost its privileged position as the compulsory language in all types of schools, primary, secondary and universities, the concept of teaching foreign laguages changed spontaneously according to the needs and motivation of students of all levels, businessmen and those involved in tourism, commerce, banking and technology, to name only a few essential areas. None of the foreign languages was given preference by the government or the Ministry of Education in the new foreign language teaching concept. Yet, in a very short time, English became the widest-spread foreign language in almost all types of schools.

This tendency of an increasing dominance of English as the first foreign language in post-Socialist Slovakia is reflected also in the results of the survey by the Department of Russian of the Faculty of Philosophy at Prešov at the beginning of the 1990s which aimed at the issue of foreign language choice in basic schools and parent priorities in selecting foreign languages for their children. Out of 490 respondents to the questionnaires 415 parents (86.5 percent) considered English as the most important language of the world; 92 percent of parents (out of 288) in the central region of Slovakia shared this opinion. As to the variety of foreign languages available at the schools, it became evident that many schools decided not even to offer Russian any longer as an option. It remains open whether this was decreed by the school administrations or whether Russian was simply ignored and totally neglected by the students.

Another research project carried out by the teachers of English in the same university department tried to analyze the situation of the teaching of the different foreign languages (Hrehovčík, 1993, 256) in Slovakia. Although the sample of respondents was relatively small, it reflected other significant changes that occured in Slovakia in the teaching of Western languages within a span of only three or four years after the collapse of the East Bloc. Statistics showed that "while in 1988/89, 80 percent of respondents had some foreign language training before they entered university, in 1992/93 each student had some experience with foreign language study. A similar tendency can be seen at primary schools where formerly 50 percent of students received foreign language education and three years later almost 74 percent". In more detail, the investigation showed that in 1989, German was the mostly taught foreign language, English was less common and French was only symbolic in primary schools. The foreign language ratio of 8 (German) : 4 (English) : 1 (French) in 1992/93, changed to 10 : 5 : 1. In the absence of further analyses, it cannot be said whether the situation has remained the same. On the secondary-school level, English has become the dominant language. The foreign-language ratio is 3 (English) : 2 (German) : 1 (French).

Research conducted among the students of the Philosophical Faculty of Prešov show the same trend. University students may study one of three or four foreign languages offered by the school. All foreign language study is optional, only a small number of students are required to take one particular language, e.g. Latin for students of history. In 1989, among all foreign languages available at the university, English was the first language (2.5), German ranked second (1), and French was on the same level. In 1992/93, the ratios became even more evident: English (13), German (10), and French (1).

The same tendencies can be found at other universities where foreign languages are taught mainly for specific purposes, e.g. at technical, economic, and veterinary universities, at military academies, medical schools, and law schools. There, the differences are even more apparent because the number of students studying individual languages is much higher. Thus, the foreign language ratio for Languages for special purposes (LSP) at the Technical University of Košice, in 1995/96, illustrates the present trend: 75 percent of students studied English, 20 percent German, and the rest took Russian or French .

One part of the investigation focused on the impact of the new socio-political situation on the students' motivation and their attitude toward foreign language courses. While before 1989 the original 40 percent of students stated that foreign language study was imperative, in 1992/93 this category of students was reduced to only 15 percent. Over one half (52.5 percent) of students still viewed foreign languages as a part of their general education. Positive motives to study foreign languages are seen in their practical use in traveling abroad (38.6 percent), for hobby and home (14,3 percent). An increasing number of students find foreign languages also important for professional reading. A radical shift in the students' attitude towards the need of foreign languages for their professional carrier is evident. Similar trends in the changes of student motivation prevail in other departments teaching English for general or special purposes.

Yet, English in all types of Slovak schools has not only been motivated by subjective factors such as travelling and studying abroad, or reading foreign literature. While, after 1989, at first general-purpose English courses were prevailing , now many ESP courses contain a Business English element as a natural part of the course. Such a shift towards English for Business, for Banking and Finance in Slovakia can be observed in other post-socialist countries in Europe. It is a reflection of the process of the vanishing of the former isolated national and state-planned markets of the socialist countries, the turn to open, free capitalist market systems and of their integration into a world market where English is the international means of communication. Economic factors prove to be the determinators in spreading English as a foreign language in Slovakia, factors which obviously are more important than political or cultural reasons, although, of course, the political, economic and cultural causes are interrelated.

IV. British and American Influences on Teaching English

The new situation of foreign languages in Slovak education brought about a number of problems. The fact that Russian ceased to be taught in most primary and secondary schools and its substitution by English, and the abrupt change in the educational policy of the country revealed a great shortage of teachers of English. This resulted into English being taught by unqualified teachers, or by teachers who, for many years, and for various reasons, had no opportunity to teach that language. The shortage in teachers of English in the country led to the hiring of a considerable number of foreign teachers mainly from the United States of America. Through the care of two organizations alone, the Education for Democracy and the Peace Corps, 1,500 volunteers have come from America to work here as teachers of English in all sorts of schools since 1990. (SAIA Bulletin, 7-8, 1)

Further problems concerned the total absence of suitable English language textbooks and the national curricula for English as a foreign language in use until 1989, which were found to be too restrictive, biased and old-fashioned.

Since 1989, English Language Teaching (ELT) in Slovakia has undergone considerable modifications which would not have been possible without the assistance and cooperation of four organizations: SAIA - SCTS (Slovak Academy Information Agency (service center for the tertiary level), the British Council, USIS (United States Information Service)

Bratislava, and SAUA/SATE (Slovak Association of English Teachers). Particularly, the close cooperation with the two non-profit institutions, the British Council and USIS, has resulted in many complex programs in the fields of methodology of teaching, teaching equipment, of teachers-of-English training. At this time, the British Council organizes six projects aimed at developing the teaching of English in Slovakia (ESP project, British Studies, Pre-Service Teacher Training, In-Service Teacher Training and English Language Teaching contacts). These projects have generated numerous related events and activities such as conferences, seminars, workshops, exhibitions, teachers-training sessions in Slovakia or in Britain.

It is impossible to enumerate all the activites organized by the British Council lecturers. But we would like to mention at least one of the highly successful projects. It is the one of the teaching methodology of English for ESP organized by Barrie Robinson and Serena Yeo advisors to Slovakia. Their enthusiasm, high competence and natural aptitude for cooperation have resulted in many seminars in various parts of Slovakia, workshops, in-service training, summer ESP courses in Trnava, Zlatá Idka, Vrútky, Sulòv, teacher training courses, networking sessions for Central Europe, training of Slovak ESP teachers in the UK, ESP conferences in Banská Bystrica and in Košice, the editing of an ESP-Newsletter (later ESP Spectrum), book and equipment donations to various Departments of English. The establishment of three very active resource centres of the British Council, offering, among others, workshops, seminars and book exhibitions, has been instrumental in the process of making English the Number One foreign language in the country.

In a similar way, a large number of seminars and workshops have been organized by lecturers of the United States Information Service (USIS) in EFL covering pre-service training, in-service training, and ESP programme. The American Sabre Foundation donated thousands of books to schools, state and university libraries.

All these programmes, some even organized internationally centered on achieving an improved teaching and learning of English, and all these activities have made a substantial impact on the methodology teaching of English in Slovak schools .

Another relatively strong influence on the dissemination of American English in Slovakia on the post-socialist foreign-language philosophy as well as on the students, teachers, and schools in the country after the fall of Communism, is today's possibility for hundreds of students from secondary schools and universities to study at educational institutions in the United States.

Firstly, such stays have considerably improved the Slovak students' command of English. Some of the students have become fluent speakers of American English. Such studies have had a highly positive feedback in the entrance examinations of the Slovak teacher-training faculties as well as in all departments where English is taught for special purposes, e.g. the departments of economics and business administration.

Secondly, at the same time, the study-abroad opportunity has caused the American version of English to gain greater popularity, a much greater one than there used to be during Socialist times when British English and British culture were favoured and dominating. Now, the younger generation are more inclined to identify with features of the American culture and way of life, such as American behavior and way of dressing. There is a strong influx of American culture via dozens of American films, fiction, magazines and journals which have a negative impact on our own culture. As Northover (1993) says "a language symbolizes favourable or unfavourable identification with members of the language group and the language is a conduit of the values of its speakers". Thus, together with the positive changes in the teaching of the English language and, in particular of its American variety we may very likely be confronted with more serious and negative implications of an American cultural and societal interference in the future.

77

Literature:

Beneš, Ed. et al.(1970) : Metodika Cizích jazyku. Praha: Státní
pedagogické nakladatelství: 9
Hrehovčík, T. (1993) : Teacher Trainees and Foreign Languages. In:
Acta Facultatis Philosophicae Universitatis Šafarikanae 10, 256-259
Marčeková, D. (1996) : Na Slovensku po anglicky 2. Elt na Slovensku -
prítomnost a budúcnost. SAUA / SATE , October 1996
Mikluš, M. (1993) : Niekol'ko slov o niektorých problémoch
cudzojazyčného vzdelávania na našich školách. In Acta: Facultatis
Philisophicae Universitatis Šafarikanae 10, 61
Northover, N. (1993) : Some Liguistic and Identity Issues in Multicul-
tural and Multilingual Societies. In: Acta Facultatis Philisophicae
Universitatis Šafarikanae 10, 298 -3O4
Pačko, J. (1993) : Vplyv rodičov na žiaka základnej školy pri vol'be
cudzieho jazyka. In: Acta Facultatis Philosophicae Universitatis
Šafarikanae 10, 71-77
Pfeil, S. (1993) : Market Society and the Use of Foreign Languages. In:
Acta Facultatis Philisophicae Universitatis Šafarikanae 10, 311
SAIA Bulletin, (1990) : Spravodaj 7-8, 1

ZUM ENGLISCHEN EINFLUSS AUF DAS HEUTIGE RUSSISCH UND TSCHECHISCH

Liane Fijas

Nicht nur in den Sprachen des früheren nicht-sozialistischen Auslandes wie dem Französisch, dem Deutsch, dem Dänisch u.a. zeigt sich besonders seit Ende des 2. Weltkrieges der angloamerikanische Einfluß in außerordentlichem Maß; in der gegenwärtigen Epoche beobachtet man auch eine übermäßige Anreicherung des lexikalischen Bestandes der russischen und der tschechischen Sprache mit Anglizismen.

Die Gründe für diese ausgesprochene linguistische Aktivität der Entlehnung aus dem Englischen, und vornehmlich dem Amerikanisch-Englischen, werden insbesondere durch politische und sozial-historische Umstände determiniert, wenn die Gesellschaft plötzlich so starken Veränderungen unterworfen wird, daß die eigene, in diesem Fall die russische Sprache, vielfach nicht mehr in der Lage ist, die neue Realität zu reflektieren. Lexikalische Leerfelder werden dann durch vorhandenes aus anderen Fremdsprachen, heutzutage in erster Linie aus der englischen Sprache stammendes Material, aufgefüllt.

Der zunehmende Einfluß der englischen Sprache auf das Russische, seit Mitte der 80er Jahre, vor allem jedoch seit Beginn der 90er Jahre und noch mehr in unseren Tagen, hat den Anteil an englischen Entlehnungen derart gesteigert, daß dieser Prozeß des „linguistic borrowing" inzwischen von fast jedem Sprachträger wahrgenommen, wenngleich nicht unbedingt auch reflektiert wird. Nach Larionova (1993, 4) übersteigt der Anglizismenstrom wesentlich den Bedarf der Lexikentwicklung der russischen Sprache und „Anglizismen beginnen die Rolle destruktiver Elemente zu spielen, die den Sprachcode unterminieren".

Am aktivsten sind dabei nach Meinung von Larionova die neuesten Anglizismen im Bereich der gesellschaftspolitischen Lexik. Diese Erscheinung wird im Zusammenhang mit den führenden Tendenzen der gesellschaftlichen Entwicklung gesehen.

Die meisten Lehnübertragungen, Lehnübersetzungen sowie Nullsubstitutionen (unveränderte Übernahme von englischem Wortgut ins Russische) entstehen dann, wenn sich neue Realia oder Begriffe in der Gesellschaft der „aufnehmenden" Sprache auszubreiten beginnen, oder, nach Ansicht des Sprechers, die Notwendigkeit der Entlehnung des angloamerikanischen Fremdwortes offensichtlich ist.
So geschah z.B. in publizistischen und schöngeistigen Texten das Eindringen bzw. die Übernahme von Wörtern aus der englischen Sprache, um ein bestimmtes nationales, geographisches, soziales oder gar politisches Kolorit zu schaffen, ein linguistisches Verfahren, das besonders charakteristisch ist für Emigrantenschriftsteller der „dritten Welle" (Larionova, 1993, 9) - **кар** (car), **сабвей** (subway). Diesem Zweck dienten auch Jargonismen englischer Herkunft, die zu bestimmten Soziolekten gehören, z.B. **герл** (girl), **прайс** (price), **баксы** (Slang: buck, Dollar) - Jargonismen der Jugendsprache (Larionova, 1993, 10).

Bis Anfang der 90er Jahre erfüllten die Anglizismen die Rolle einer ideologisch markierten Lexik in einer Situation des politischen Widerstandes. In der Semantik des englischen Lehngutes, das sozial oder politisch bedeutsame Erscheinungen und Begriffe der Realität anderer Länder bezeichnete, verbanden sich Besonderheiten der ideologischen mit exotischer Lexik. Im Vergleich zu den Prototypen der Anglizismen in der russischen Sprache bildeten sich, je nach dem semantischen Potential des Wortes, zusätzliche semantische Schattierungen und Nuancierungen, vor allem jedoch eine beständig negative Konnotation heraus. Bei den englischsprachigen Entlehnungen, die negative Erscheinungen und Begriffe bezeichnen, wurde die national-kulturelle Komponente,

„verbreitet in kapitalistischen Ländern - in England, den USA" umgedeutet in das Ideologische, „verbreitet in der bürgerlichen Gesellschaft". Das wiedrum fand seinen Ausdruck in den Wortdefinitionen, z.B. стагфляция „Stillstand, Rezession, Abfall in der kapitalistischen Wirtschaft, begleitet durch Inflation" (Larionova, 1993, 10) (vgl. engl. stagflation „..... to describe the previously unprecedented combination of slow economic growth and high unemployment (stagnation) with rising prices (inflation)" (Friedman, 1994, 575).

Seit Mitte der 80er Jahre verschwand im Zusammenhang mit den Veränderungen der sozial-politischen Verhältnisse der Bedarf an ideologischen Exotismen. Man begann die Anglizismen mit Bezug auf die veränderte Wirklichkeit in den GUS-Staaten anzuwenden. Englisches in der russischen Sprache verlor seine stereotype ideologisch gefärbte Konnotation.

Derzeit ist die Entlehnung englischen Wortgutes durch eine Reihe charakteristischer Merkmale gekennzeichnet:

Thematisch überwiegt angloamerikanische gesellschaftlich-wirtschaftliche Lexik, hervorgerufen aus kulturell historischen und sozial-historischen Gründen und andererseits begründet in einer für alle europäischen Sprachen geltenden Entlehnungstendenz. Fragen der Wirtschaft stehen nicht nur in den post-sozialistischen Ländern, aber doch ganz besonders dort im Mittelpunkt der gesellschaftlichen Aufmerksamkeit. Das führt insbesondere zur Übernahme der englischen, sprich amerikanischen Wirtschaftsterminologie. (Larionova, 1993, 12). Englische Wörter, thematisch miteinander verbunden, gehen gleichzeitig in die russische Sprache ein, gleichsam als Block, wobei sie sich in lexikalisch semantische und thematische Mikrosysteme gruppieren, z.B. **маркетинг** (marketing) und **менеджмент** (management) oder **брокер** (broker) und **дистирибьютор** (distributor) und **дилер** (dealer).
Дилер (dealer) erhält die Bedeutung „Businessman, Händler". Außerdem wird auch noch eine spezielle Bedeutung des Anglizismus „dealer"

entlehnt, nämlich „Verkaufsagent", was dem russischen Wort „**дистрибьютор**" nahekommt - eine Person (Firma) also, die den Absatz auf der Basis von Großhandelseinkäufen realisiert (Larionova, 1993, 13).

Larionova nennt 3 Typen von Entlehnungen aus dem Englischen (Larionova, 1993, 14):

1. Am weitesten verbreitet und am besten beschrieben ist der Entlehnungstyp, der durch kulturellen Einfluß bedingt ist, wenn englische Wörter gemeinsam mit den Realia (Begriffen), die sich in der Gesellschaft etablieren, in die Sprache gelangen, z.B. **холдинг** (= Holding) oder **ноу-хау** (Know-how).

2. Ein zweiter Typ von Entlehnungen umfaßt Anglizismen, die ins Russische durch die Bezeichnung von Erscheinungen gelangen, die in der Gesellschaft zwar existieren, aber noch keine eigene Benennung in der Sprache haben, wie z.B. **бартер** (= barter) oder **бизнесвумен** (=business woman).

3. Der dritte Entlehnungstyp wird als neuer und vorläufig noch nicht charakteristischer Typ betrachtet. Es handelt sich um die Entlehnung englischsprachiger Lexik zur Schaffung von neuen Wörtern auf russischer Basis. So wurde z.B. **ваучер** (= voucher) als „Dokument, das als Zahlungsmittel gegen Waren und Dienstleistungen ausgetauscht werden kann", (Larionova, 1993, 14) in die russische Sprache lehnübertragen zur Benennung einer neuen russischen Erscheinung, nämlich „Privatisierungscheck". Entlehnungen dieses Typs sind allerdings selten auf Grund einer ähnlichen Semantik.

Die Tatsache, daß es im Russischen für bestimmte Erscheinungen kein sprachliches Äquivalent gibt, zwingt unter Umständen zur Übernahme von Anglizismen.

Ein Beispiel ist **спонсор** (= sponsor). Im Russischen gab es dafür lediglich den Archaismus **меценат** - „reicher Wohltäter der Wissenschaften und Künste" (Larionova, 1993, 14). Aus den Archaismen der russischen Sprache ist das Wort gleichsam in den Gegenwartswortschatz zurückgekehrt. Während im Russischen somit zwei Wörter, ein englisches und ein russisches nebeneinander bestehen, verdrängt der Anglizismus **спонсор** das Synonym **меценат** jedoch immer mehr, da der Anglizismus eher dem Charakter unserer modernen Zeit entspricht und darüberhinaus nicht nur auf eine Person, sondern auch auf einen Betrieb, eine Firma, ein Wirtschaftsunternehmen, anwendbar ist (Larionova, 1993, 15). Diesem semantischen Anspruch kann der „zurückgekehrte" Archaismus **меценат** nicht mehr genügen.

Beobachtungen zur Sozialisierung der neuesten Anglizismen haben gezeigt, daß die Etablierung und Integrierung von Anglizismen im aktiven Wortschatz der Träger der russischen Sprache von der sozialen Bedeutsamkeit des Denotats und der Vorkommenshäufigkeit des Wortes in den Massenmedien abhängt. Es besteht eine enge und dynamische Verbindung zwischen den Prozessen der Sozialisierung, der semantischen Anpassung und der Entwicklung der Anglizismen in der russischen Sprache (Larionova, 1993, 16).

Dennoch bleiben die inzwischen offensichtlich zum Problem gewordenen englisch-russischen Sprachkontakte auch weiterhin ein noch unzureichend erforschter Bereich der Sprachwissenschaft.

Das bereits eingangs aufgezeigte intensive Eindringen englischen Wortgutes in die russische Sprache seit den 80er Jahren mag einerseits durch die gesellschaftlichen Umwälzungen in Rußland und die daraus resultierenden neuen wirtschaftlichen Gegebenheiten bedingt sein.

Andererseits liegen die Gründe sicher auch in den rasanten Entwicklungen in vielen Wissenschaftsgebieten, u.a. in der Kommunikations- und Computertechnik, und in der ständig zunehmenden Globalisierung des Wirtschaftslebens. Ländergrenzen für sprachliche Neologismen werden heute viel schneller überschritten als noch vor zwei Jahrzehnten, als es neben den physischen noch die ideologischen Grenzen des kalten Kriges gab. Darüberhinaus zwingen in der bisher rückständigen, nunmehr der sogenannten freien Marktwirtschaft zugewandten russischen Wirtschaft scheinbare Bezeichnungsdefizite manchmal geradezu zur schnellen Übernahme von englischem Wortgut.

Noch vor Jahrzehnten durchlief dieser Prozeß der Entlehnung mindestens folgende Schritte:

- Das fremde Wort tritt in enge Wechselwirkung mit bereits vorhandenen eigenständigen Wörtern, aber es ist im System der russischen Sprache noch nicht semantisch „etabliert" und noch nicht von seinem englischen Ursprung losgelöst, um einen selbständigen Platz im Kreis der bedeutungsverwandten heimischen Wörter einzunehmen;

- Das fremde Wort erfährt eine Art Erprobung seiner Notwendigkeit als Entlehnung in die russische Sprache, eine Art Entscheidung über den Einschluß des englischen Wortes in das russische Sprachsystem und eine Reaktion der dort bereits vorhandenen Wörter. Das Resultat ist entweder die Entlehnung oder Ablehnung des Anglizismus oder aber ein zeitweiliges oder andauerndes Nebeneinander von englischem und russischem Wort mit oder ohne sozio- und/oder psycholinguistischer Gewichtung.

- Es kann zu semantischen Verschiebungen in den Ursprungswörtern kommen, die in ihrer Bedeutung ähnlich sind oder anfänglich absolut synonyme Wörter darstellen, Einschränkungen des Bedeutungsumfanges eines Ursprungswortes, stilistische Markierungen und andere semantische Veränderungen stimulieren oder die Entlehnung des einen oder anderen Wortes ausschließen.

Heute lassen sich diese Schritte vermutlich auf die Formel reduzieren: neue Erscheinung/Erfindung → Bezeichnungsdefizit in der eigenen Sprache → ausländisches, (in der Regel englisches) Wort bereits vorhanden, da neue Technologie im englischsprachigen Raum entstanden → schnelle Bezeichnungsübernahme angestrebt.

Als gutes Beispiel zur Entstehung bzw. Übernahme neuer Wörter im Computerjargon, weisen Brejdo und Hartung auf das tiefe Eindringen von englischem Wortgut in die russische Sprache hin. Die überwiegende Mehrheit der neuen Wörter entsteht dabei durch direkte Entlehnung (Nullsubstitution) oder Transliteration; Lehnprägungen, wie card-programme computer **вычислительное устройство с перфокартомным управлением** oder Lehnübersetzungen, wie byte-organized computer **вычислителная машина с байтовой организацией** sind seltener (Brejdo/Hartung, 1997, 302).
Noch zu Beginn des 18. Jahrhunderts wurden bei der Erweiterung des russischen Wortschatzes die Bezeichnungslücken „unter Nutzung aller derivativer Möglichkeiten des *russischen Sprachsystems* durch neue *russische* Wörter geschlossen. Es setzte ein allseitiger Wortschöpfungsprozeß ein, der in erster Linie von den Sprachträgern befördert wurde" (Brejdo/Hartung, 1997, 302). Diesem Verfahren hat offensichtlich der Einfluß Amerikas ein Ende gesetzt.

Die Autoren verweisen in ihrem Beitrag auf die Entstehung eines speziellen Soziolekts im Russischen, eines Jargons für Computerfachleute, Informatiker und Computerhändler. Nach ihrer Ansicht stellt dieser Soziolekt ein spezifisches 'Schutzschild' gegen eine

Überfremdung der russischen Fachsprache durch das Angloamerikanische in diesem Kommunikationsbereich dar. So wird im Computerjargon beispielsweise aus 'Pentium' **пентюк**', aus 'CD-ROM' **сидюшник**' Brejdo/Hartung, 1997, 302).

Zur Illustration sei folgender Dialog aus dem Beitrag wiedergegeben (Brejdo/Hartung, 1997, 302)

- Два юзера:
- Ты в Ворде работаешь?
- В Ворде, в чем же еще?
- Не забывай каждый раз сейфовать все файлы,
  а то он часто виснет.
- Да я сейфую. А ты броузеришь?
- Брауэерю, да наш вебмастер время считает, как зверь.

Die deutsche Übersetzung des Dialogs ist insofern schwierig, als sie nicht alle Feinheiten der Sprache widerzuspiegeln vermag. Zumindest soll sie im folgenden aber versucht werden.

- Arbeitest Du in <u>Word?</u>
- In <u>Word</u>, wo sonst?
- Vergiß nicht, jedesmal alle <u>Files</u> zu <u>safen</u>, sonst
  stürzt er ab.
- Ja ich <u>safe</u>. Und <u>browst</u> Du auch?
- Ich <u>browse</u> , und unser <u>Webmaster</u> zählt die Zeit wie
  ein wildes Tier.
  (d.h. es können hohe Kosten anfallen.)

Solche Computerjargonismen können oft nur von Insidern verstanden werden, wie die nachstehenden Gegenüberstellungen zeigen: so sind Jargonismen, z.B.:

1. **хард/ железо** für hardware;
2. **писишка/ писюшка/ писюк** für PC;
3. **пятерка/ пентюх/ пентоид** für Pentium;
4. **мама/ мамка/ матка/ матушка** für motherboard;
5. **винды** für Windows;
6. **сейфовать** für speichern (von „to save"),

denen teilweise rein englischen die russischen Normentermini gegenüber-
stehen:

1. **аппаратные средства;**
2. PC;
3. pentium (**пентиум**)
4. motherboard;
5. Windows;
6. **сохранить, спасти**

Während es in Rußland kaum Bestrebungen gibt, etwas gegen den starken
englischen Einfluß und die rasante Integration von Anglizismen,
insbesondere in der Wirtschaftssphäre und der Sprache der Werbung, zu
unternehmen, hat diese sprachliche und natürlich auch kulturelle
Interferenz, in manchen ehemaligen sozialistischen Ländern starken
Widerstand gezeigt.

Die Sprache kennt keine Ländergrenzen! So werden
auch alle Versuche „staatlich gesteuerten Sprachpurismus" zu betreiben, wahrscheinlich nicht zu den
erwarteten Ergebnissen führen. Ähnlich den Fran-
zosen, die um die scheinbar schlechten Einflüsse,
insbesondere des Angloamerikanischen auf die Französische Sprache besorgt sind, führen nun auch die
Slowaken mit einem seit Januar 1997 geltenden Gesetz über die Staatssprache ähnliche Sanktionen ein.

Quelle: Die Karpatenpost, Februar 1997, S. 16

Mickey Mouse
künftig in der Slowakei tabu

In der Slowakei wird es künftig keine „Shops" mehr
geben und kein „Bodybuilding" - Studio. „Mickey
Mouse" und ihre Verwandten werden für Kinder eben-
so tabu sein wie beliebte tschechische Märchenvideos.
Seit dem 1. Januar gelten nämlich Sanktionen, die das
vor einem Jahr erlassene Gesetz über die Staatssprache
vorsieht. Nun werden „Sprachinspekteure" des Kul-
tusministeriums darüber wachen, daß die Slowaken in
der Öffentlichkeit keine Amerikanismen benutzen, daß
einem f remdsprachigen Text stets eine slowakische
Übersetzung voransteht. Vor allem aber dürfen sich An-
gehörige der starken ungarischen Minderheit auf Ämtern
untereinander nicht mehr in ihrer Muttersprache unterhal-
ten. Das auch im Ausland kritisierte Gesetz, das auch
Staatspräsident Michal Kovac zu verhindern suchte, wird
unter anderem als Akt der Abgrenzung zu Tschechien
gesehen. Eigentliche Zielrichtung aber scheint die ungarische Minderheit im Süden des Landes zu sein, die immer-
hin gut 10 Prozent des Staatsvolkes ausmacht. In ihren
Schulen und Medien dürfen ungarische Texte nur noch
verwendet werden, wenn sie zuvor in slowakischer Sprache
vorgelegen haben. Der Amtsverkehr in den ungarisch domi-
nierten Gemeindeverwaltungen darf nur noch auf slowa-
kisch erfolgen.   Klaus Martin, dpa
Aus der Filderzeitung, 4.1.1997.

Es gibt zahlreiche Beispiele im täglichen Leben und in den unterschiedlichsten Bereichen, die den nachhaltigen Einfluß des Englischen auch auf das Tschechische bzw. das Slowakische reflektieren. Besonders betroffen sind offenbar die Printmedien, wie nachfolgend einige Beispiele zeigen sollen. Vielleicht ist es auch eher der „blinde" oder „bewußte" Journalismus, der durch die Übernahme immer neuen und mitunter bis zur totalen Adaption an das Sprachsystem reichenden Wortgutes besonders „In" sein oder insbesondere viele jüngere Leser „erreichen" will? Dabei sind die Slowaken, zumindest die slowakischen Kulturbehörden, offensichtlich der Meinung, daß wenigstens ein bewußterer Umgang mit der eigenen Sprache und die kritische Auseinandersetzung mit Spracheinflüssen vor einer blinden Übernahme von neuem angloamerikanischen Wortgut stehen sollte.

Auch im heutigen Tschechisch treten im wesentlichen 3 Gruppen von Entlehnungen englischen Sprachgutes auf:

1. Direkte Entlehnung - Nullsubstitutionen, wie:

leasing	boom
product manager	minitest
inline	minitower
medical sales representatives	software
labourist	super (super cena = Superpreis)
client	slogan
server	megastar Michael Jackson
(americký) gentleman	supertramp
video	internet

2. Teilsubstitutionen

Viele englische Ausdrücke werden nicht einfach im Original, also als Nullsubstitution übernommen, sondern als Mischung von Englischem und Tschechischem bzw. als Lehnübertragung. Sie werden damit gleichsam „tschechisiert", d.h., den phonologischen, morphologischen und syntaktischen Regeln der tschechischen Sprache unterworfen. Die folgenden Beispiele verdeutlichen insbesondere die morphologisch-syntaktische Anpassung der Amerikanismen an die tschechische Sprache.

.... mluvči newsweek**u**   (Gen., Sg.)

supermarket**ům**   (Dativ Pl.)

multímedi**ální**   (Adj.!)   (= multimedia)

moderni trend**y**   (Pl.)

windovs 95 CZ

.... o **cornflacich** nechci ani slyšet ....   (cornflakes)

.... **recyklovátelné** obaly ....   (recyclingfähige Verpackungen)
   (recyclable)

leasing**ový** - **ová**, - **ové**   (Adj.)

labourist - **ská**, **-ské**   (Adj.)

oder dealerů společnosti ...   (von Vertretern der Gesellschaft)

dealer**ový** - **ová**, - **ové**   (Adj.)

teenager**ům**

video → vide**a**

.... pro oblast softwar**ové** podpory

broker → Pl. broke**ři**   (broker); (so auch mákler - Pl. makle**ři** aus dem Deutschen)

minimotocy**kl**; minibike

adapt**ér**

subsyst**ém**

jeho čeká **sexproces**

Ve stostránkovém hit**u** letošního léta najdete.....

Kazeta nebo kompakt (= cassette or compact disk)

v tandemu

velký boom (economic boom)

handicap**ované** děti (= handicapped children)

deregulace; aber auch: deregulation!

rap s rokem (Rap with Rock)

marketing**ová** (agent**ura**) (marketing agency)

škola **snou**boarding**u** (= snowboarding school)

škola **snou**board**ista** (= snowboarding school)

safari styl (= safari style/ looke) (Dávám přednost třeba safari stylu)

3. Eine dritte Gruppe von Wörtern englischer Herkunft, die bereits
    vollkommen im tschechischen Sprachsystem assimiliert sind und von
    das Tschechische nicht beherrschenden Personen oft nicht mehr als
    fremd bzw. als Anglizismus erkannt werden, sind Entlehnungen wie:

byznys (= business)

na minulém **šampionátu** (= championship) ve Vídní

vlastní gól (= goal)

gólman (= goal keeper)

hledáme na **pozice** (= position) personalista

kouč (= coach); Hokejisté Liberece maji třetiho kouč**e**

čipová karta (= chip card)

tradovat (= to trade);

manažer (= manager)

manažérka (= manageress)

aber auch: manager

fanoušek, Gen. fanoušků (= fan)

neférový trénink (= unfair training)

džínsy (= jeans)

Heute beobachten wir einen gewaltigen Spracheinfluß Amerikas auch auf die früher sprachlich eher abgeschotteten Ostblockländer. Dies gilt einerseits für die bereitwillige Aufnahme und den Import von Amerikanisch-Englischem Wortgut, insbesondere aber für die Akzeptanz der durch sie bezeichneten Produkte, Ideen und Lebensweisen.

Wie im Westen, wo nur ein Land „Sprachwiderstand" leistet, so ist es auch im Osten im Grunde nur ein Land, nämlich die Slowakei, wo solche Tendenzen zu verfolgen sind.

Ob man dabei von wirklichem „Sprachpurismus" oder nur von Sorge um den Erhalt der Muttersprache und der auch von ihr begründeten Kultur sprechen kann, muß die Zukunft zeigen.

Die Interferenz des Amerikanismus - sprachlich, soziologisch oder auch psychologisch - wie gelegentlich der Fall, als amerikanischen Kulturimperialismus zu belegen, dürfte schwer sein und zumindest das Phänomen nicht eindämmen oder beseitigen. Letzlich zeigt die Entwicklung, daß in der Regel auch die postsozialistischen Sprachgemeinschaften den Amerikanismus - bewußt oder unbewußt - bereitwillig aufnehmen, pflegen und weiterentwickeln.

92

Literatur:

Friedman, Jack P. (1994): Dictionary of Business Terms. Second Edition, Barron's Business Guides, USA

Larionova, Elena, V. (1993): Novejšie anglicizmy v sovremennom russkom jazyke (na materiale obščestvenno - ékonomičeskoj leksiki), Special'nost' 10.02.01 russkij jazyk; Avtoreferat dissertacii na soiskanie učenoj stepeni kandidata fililogičeskich nauk, Moskva

Aristova, Valentina, M. (1980): Anglo-russkie jazykovye kontakty i zaimstrovanija XVI - XX vv., 10.02.01 - russkij jazyk, Avtoreferat dissertacii na soiskanie učenoj stepeni doktora filologičeskich nauk, Leningrad

Brejdo, Jewgenij und Hartung, Jürgen (1997): Russischer Computerjargon In: Fremdsprachenunterricht 4/1997, 302 - 303

Die Verfasser und Herausgeber:

Mária Pešeková, PhD.	Department of Languages and Humanities
	TU Vysokoškolska č 4
	04001 Košice/ Slovak Republic
Mgr. Otília Venková	Katedra cizích jazyků
	TU Vysoká Skola Bànská,
	Katedra jazyků, Dr. Malèho 17
	702 00 Ostrava 2
	Czech Republic
Dr. Marcela Adámková	Katedra cizích jazyků
	TU Vysoká Skola Bànská,
	Katedra jazyků, Dr. Malèho 17
	702 00 Ostrava 2
	Czech Republic
Prof. Mari Uibo	Director of Modern Languages
	TTU Tallinn, Estonia
	Department of Modern Languages
	Ehitajate tee 5
	Tallinn EE 0028
Dr. Viera Nemčoková	Department of Languages and Humanities
	TU Vysokoškolska č. 4
	04001 Košice/ Slovak Republic
Dr. Gabriela Knutová	Department of Languages and Humanities
	TU Vysokoškolska č. 4
	04001 Košice/ Slovak Republic
Dr. Liane Fijas	Direktorin, Universitätssprachenzentrum
	TU Bergakademie Freiberg
	Lessingstraße 45
	09596 Freiberg
Prof. Dr. Hermann Fink	Zur Imburg 15
	33165 Lichtenau-Herbram

**Freiberger Beiträge zum Einfluß
der angloamerikanischen Sprache und Kultur auf Europa**

Herausgegeben von Hermann Fink und Liane Fijas

Band 1   Andrea Effertz/Ulrike Vieth: Das Verständnis wirtschaftsspezifischer Anglizismen in der deutschen Sprache bei Unternehmern, Führungskräften und Mitarbeitern der neuen und alten Bundesländer. 1996.

Band 2   Thorsten Bagschik: Utopias in the English-speaking World and the Perception of Economic Reality. 1996.

Band 3   Hermann Fink: Von *Kuh-Look* bis *Fit for Fun*: Anglizismen in der heutigen deutschen Allgemein- und Werbesprache. 1997.

Band 4   Hermann Fink/Liane Fijas/Danielle Schons: Anglizismen in der Sprache der Neuen Bundesländer. Eine Analyse zur Verwendung und Rezeption. 1997.

Band 5   Hermann Fink/Liane Fijas (Eds.): America and Her Influence upon the Language and Culture of Post-socialist Countries. 1998.